*Color exists not as applied paint
but as the inner core of
an idea and this idea cannot
be touched physically any more
than one can touch the blue
of a summer sky.*

BEN NICHOLSON

CONRAN
ON
COLOR

Terence Conran

conran
OCTOPUS

To Jill Webb,
who played such an energetic
role in putting together the
Conran paint range.
Thank you, Jill, and your
colorful team.

CONTENTS

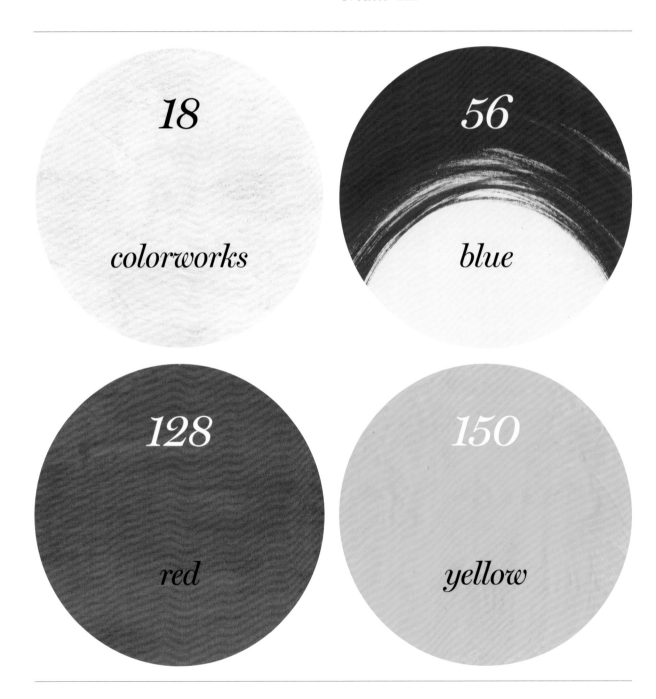

18

colorworks

56

blue

128

red

150

yellow

84 *orange*

104 *green*

168 *naturals*

190 *neutrals*

introduction

introduction

Color is one of the most dynamic elements in design and decoration. Even its absence makes its presence felt. Subtle and allusive or bold and invigorating, there's nothing like it to add spice to life and soul to your surroundings.

A key reason for this inherent strength and energy is the raft of associations that colors bring in their wake. These may be as subjective as a personal memory of a place or a favorite object, or as shared as cultural meanings. Certain shades may summon up the signature palette of a well-known artist or designer ("Titian red"), or a specific landscape or region, or pinpoint a moment in time. Color can even be a brand. Added to which, by virtue of the way they are perceived, different colors naturally provoke feelings, moods, and sensations, from the distancing and soothing effect of blues, to the restfulness of greens, to the siren call of reds. The language of color is rich and layered.

NATURE

It's hardly surprising that so many names we commonly give to colors, from coral to eggplant to cornflower blue, make reference to things that live and grow. Nature has always been a huge source of color inspiration for me, as it has been for so many others, whether it comes in the form of a neat, well-tended vegetable plot, a wild-flower meadow, or the sun-drenched landscape of the south of France, with its azure sea, lavender fields and purple-green vineyards. As a child, I was passionate about butterflies and entranced by the striking patterns on their wings.

The colors in nature are both varied and vivid. Yet it is worth remembering that nature can be very subtle, too—think of the delicate gray-green of buds in spring, or pale primrose yellow. Using color successfully doesn't always mean reaching for the boldest, brightest shade in the paintbox. Quieter, more contemplative schemes, where the color relationships shift as the light changes throughout the day, can have equal depth and character.

Many people who fight shy of strong color resort to pastels instead—commonly available as tonal versions of brighter shades with a lot of white mixed in. Pastel schemes are often overly demure—watered down to the extent that all life has been sucked out of them. A much better option, if you are after a light palette, would be to seek out those pale, interesting shades that hover on the edge of one color and the next—colors such as celadon, dove gray, and lilac. Containing both warm and cool elements, these complex tones are extremely evocative.

ART

Inspiration can also come from the work of those who have a great eye for color—painters, photographers, fashion designers, and graphic artists. I am particularly drawn to faded, bleached shades, and the subtleties of color in Ben Nicholson's work have always attracted me.

One of the supreme colorists of the 20th century was Henri Matisse, whose late works in cut-out paper are exercises in the pure pleasure of color—they positively vibrate. When I was a student, I worked for a time in Zika Ascher's print studio in Shepherd Market, London.

Ascher was a textile designer and producer, whose 'Artists' Squares' featured the work of leading contemporary artists, from Henry Moore to Graham Sutherland. These overscaled scarves were intended as wearable art, but most people who bought them stapled them to frames and hung them on their walls instead. One of Ascher's best-known collaborations was with Matisse, and it was his *Océanie* wall panels that I was privileged to work on. The linen cloth was a specific shade of grayish beige, intended to replicate the color of Matisse's bedroom walls—by that time the artist was bedridden and his bedroom was effectively his studio. The white cut-out shapes were screen-printed on the cloth. I was sorely tempted to make a mistake with the registration so that I could have my own Matisse to take home. The panels were produced in a limited edition of 30 and are now museum pieces.

TECHNOLOGY

Given the way nature bursts with color of every shade and hue, it must have been intensely frustrating to our ancestors that they were not able to reproduce what they saw around them every day in the form of pigments and dyestuffs. Over the centuries, the story of color has been one of trial and error, dead ends and happy accident. Who could have predicted that one of the strongest reds might come from the carapaces of crushed female beetles, or that a pure, heavenly blue might be derived from a mineral found almost exclusively in a remote region of Afghanistan? Until fairly recently in human history, colors were hard won, often toxic and fugitive, and sometimes astronomically expensive.

Color has never been so accessible, achievable, or economical as it is today. The emergence of synthetic dyes and pigments in the middle of the 19th century started the ball rolling. Ready-mixed artists' colors in portable tubes meant painters could work out of doors, propping canvases in front of their sources of inspiration, a plein-air movement that lead directly to Impressionism. The years immediately following World War II saw developments in the petrochemical industry that brought color to the mass-market as never before. What had once been rare and prized was now cheap, cheerful, and everywhere.

PAINT BY CONRAN

The paint business runs in the family. My father was an importer of gum copal, which was used to make paints and varnishes—the resin was dug out of swamps in what was then the Belgian Congo and often had insects embedded in it. After an air raid destroyed the firm's premises during World War II, my father worked for a paint company and helped to advise Hertfordshire architects on which paint colors to choose for schools. One of my own earliest color memories was opening a kitchen cabinet and dislodging a tin of green paint that spilled all over the terra cotta floor. I thought the clash of colors was absolutely disgusting.

In the early days of Habitat we had our own paint range featuring the type of colors—Chinese red, for example—that manufacturers did not then produce and which appealed to a new market of young people, who wanted to be more daring in their interiors. At that time, if you wanted an unusual color to paint your walls, you had to mix it yourself or find someone to do it for you.

So I am particularly delighted that the opportunity has now arisen to launch a new Paint by Conran range in collaboration with a firm that has been manufacturing paint for more than 120 years. Our partners, Master Paintmakers, produce paint of a very high quality and technical specification—salt-resistant paint for lighthouses, for example, or paint that can withstand 7 inches of stretching when a supersonic jet breaks the sound barrier.

British plant life and landscapes are the inspiration behind the range, from the tweedy purples and slate grays of the Highlands of Scotland to the powder blues and poppy reds of a typical English cottage garden. Nature, as always, remains the ultimate touchstone.

PART ONE **COLORWORKS**

THE
SCIENCE
OF
COLOR

Left A group of glass vases filled with flowers on the oak dining table in our London flat. The Wishbone chairs were designed by Hans Wegner in 1949. On the wall is a photograph of Kyoto in Japan by the Austrian-born artist Gerd Hasler.

Below One of my gray blue shirts hanging in our compact fitted wardrobe—along with some of my wife's bright red accessories.

Like many people, I suppose, I had never given too much thought to the science of color. I was aware that different colors correspond to different wavelengths of light, as first demonstrated by Sir Isaac Newton in his experiments with prisms. But I am a designer, not a physicist, and my preoccupation has always been with color's impact on our surroundings and its overall role in design. So I was absolutely fascinated to read an account recently that set out the science in greater detail.

Contrary to appearances, color is not a property of objects, it's the way our minds make sense of how our eyes perceive light. A red apple isn't red, any more than grass is green. What is actually going on is that when light falls on an apple that we see as "red," all the wavelengths of light except the red are absorbed, while the red is reflected back to us. Color is, therefore, akin to energy or vibration.

The visible spectrum occupies only a minute proportion of the electromagnetic waves that make up the universe. But within the narrow range of these wavelengths we can detect many millions of subtle variations—it is estimated that we can distinguish between thousands of shades of white and near-white alone.

COLOR THEORY IN ACTION

Left Few color statements come stronger than this. The glossy yellow panels covering a wall of built-in storage, the red spines of the shelved books, and the bright blue upholstery of the chair show the power of primary shades in action. There is enough neutral space in the room to mediate.

Below These sheets of paper, pinned to the wall of my study, show my experiments with different color combinations. A key factor when combining colors is the proportion in which they are used.

Our response to color is deeply subjective. You don't need to be an expert in color theory to be drawn to a particular shade. It gets a little trickier, however, when you come to put different colors together in an interior.

Knowing which colors are naturally harmonious, which are dynamic in combination, and which fight with each other will help you come up with richer and more powerful decorative schemes. For this you need to understand the basics of color relationships.

The classic way of representing color relationships is the artist's color wheel. When light passes through a prism it reveals a continuous spectrum of color. The color wheel —which is basically an abstract construction—represents the spectrum as six distinct bands brought round to join in a circle: red, violet, blue, green, yellow, and orange.

Primary colors
Red, blue, and yellow cannot be created by mixing any other colors together. In their purest form, they are arresting and graphic.

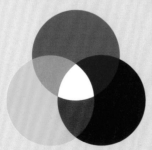

Secondary colors
These are made by mixing adjacent primary colors. Purple, or violet, is a blend of blue and red, green a blend of yellow and blue, and orange a blend of red and yellow.

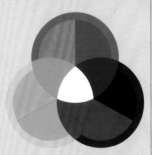

Tertiary colors
Composed of an equal mixture of a primary and a secondary color, tertiary colors, such as turquoise, hover on the edge.

Complementary colors
Colors that sit opposite each other on the color wheel are naturally electrifying. These pairings—red and green, blue and orange, and yellow and purple—almost seem to vibrate next to each other.

LIGHT
AND
COLOR

Left These vivid sliding panels of textured glass, used to screen a bathroom, make a glowing focal point—a contemporary version of stained glass.

Below The all-white bedroom in our London flat is bathed with natural light from the window wall overlooking the River Thames. There's no better way to wake up in the morning than to see light reflected on the water.

NATURAL LIGHT

The quality of natural light has a profound effect on how we perceive color in the interior. For this reason, I generally advise people to live with the blank slate of white or off-white walls for a while, to give them time to assess the lighting conditions in different areas in the home and how they fluctuate during the course of the day.

✳
Aspect, or orientation, is the key factor to consider. In the northern hemisphere, rooms that face south or west are naturally warmer than those that face north or east (and vice versa in the southern hemisphere). For this reason, the same blue that can be fresh and uplifting in a south-facing space might be downright chilly and depressing in a north-facing one.

✳
Light levels also have a bearing. On a clear, sunny day, the light level by a window indoors may be as little as a tenth of what it is outside, and this will decrease the further you go from the window. A typical row house, with windows only at the front and back, often has a dark central core. This can be alleviated by installing some top-lighting or by using mirrors to bounce light around.

✳
Edgy shades, such as greeny blue, eggplant, and various shades of gray, tend to shift in appearance more noticeably than many other colors when light levels vary at different times of the day, adding inherent vitality to decorative schemes.

Below Under-lighting built-in cabinets helps to dematerialize their bulk. Recessed halogen spotlights produce a clean, white light that is ideal for carrying out kitchen tasks.

Right Tungsten light sources have a warm cast that is very hospitable and easy on the eye. The slotted design of these large pendants diffuses the light and creates a soft, intimate glow that is ideal for the dining table.

ARTIFICIAL LIGHT

Natural light is the benchmark by which all forms of artificial light are judged. While daylight is deemed "white," artificial light sources all have distinct color casts in comparison.

❊ The familiar tungsten bulb produces a warm, yellowish light that is only slightly cooler than candlelight and firelight. In many parts of the world, this light source is being phased out in favour of more energy-efficient sources —although there are some, myself included, who prefer the more intimate light emitted by a tungsten bulb.

❊ Halogen, both household power and low-voltage, produces a crisp, white light much closer to daylight. This is an advantage in areas of the home, such as kitchens and work rooms, where fine color judgements must be made.

❊ Fluorescent light sources have improved a great deal. In the past they had a typically greenish cast that deadened the atmosphere and looked a little sickly. Modern versions remain coolish in appearance but are closer to white.

Color effects

❊

Shining light through a transparent or translucent material is a good way of enhancing its quality. Options include:

❊

Frosted, etched, or stained glass in windows or doors.

❊

Backlit, translucent, colored Perspex panels.

❊

Colored fabric or paper lampshades.

❊

Unlined drapes, lace ,or gauzy window treatments.

❊

Fiber optics, where light is directed down thin fiberglass or acrylic strands from a remote source, can be used to light water atmospherically. So, too, can light-emitting diodes (LEDs).

ENHANCING
SPACE

Left Using color is an unbeatable way of both enhancing and defining space. Bright acid-green marks out a compact work station built into a mezzanine level, transforming it into an architectural detail.

Below Red and green are complementary shades and exceptionally powerful in combination. These contrasting doors and panels make full use of this inherent dynamism.

In tandem with light, color plays an important role in defining and enhancing space—making the most of assets and downplaying drawbacks. Again, it is worth living with a fairly neutral palette for a while before committing yourself.

PROVIDING UNITY

It is generally a good idea to plan a color scheme for your home as a whole, rather than approach decoration in a piecemeal fashion. This is certainly the case when considering large investments—for example, flooring, kitchen cabinets, and work surfaces, or upholstered furniture—which are not as simple or economical to change as a paint finish. Picking a family of colors that will crop up here and there throughout your home is a great way of providing unity. This is not to say that every room should be decorated in exactly the same way, but that there should

be some sort of thread of continuity that holds everything together. The smaller the space at your disposal, the more important this is.

Don't just think in terms of wall color. Floors also occupy a large surface area, and their color and material have a great impact on the overall mood of a space. Laying the same type of flooring throughout your home is a subtle way of providing visual coherence. Where basic practicality dictates a change of material—from pale wood to water-resistant tile, for example, keeping the two tonally similar will deliver the same effect.

DEFINING AREAS

In houses or homes that are comprised of a number of self-contained rooms, there is little need for spatial definition—the doors do that for you. But in open-plan spaces, which many homes these days tend to have, color can be a useful way of signaling a shift of activity or of helping to anchor furniture placement.

The "feature" wall is a classic example of this. A wall painted a strong or evocative color can form the backdrop to an eating area within an open-plan living space. The same is true of a built-in work station picked out in a vibrant shade —color helps to make sense of the architectural feature and in some sense justify its presence. Even more simply, a large, colorful rug will tie together a grouping of seat furniture, which otherwise might seem to float a little in space.

ADJUSTING SCALE AND VOLUME

Color can go some way to adjusting our perception of a space that is less than perfectly proportioned.

* Airy, distancing colors that lead the eye onwards help to push back the walls in narrow, cramped spaces.
* Striped wallpaper or wallpaper with a strong vertical emphasis adds visual height if ceilings are low.
* Where ceilings are disproportionately high compared to the floor area, paneling or horizontal bands of color painted on the wall will help to lower them.

Below The painted interiors of these built-in alcove beds define a sense of ownership and belonging, which is very important when children are sharing a room. The large storage drawer underneath provides useful stowing space.

Right Within open-plan layouts or built-in spaces, color is a very useful way of signaling a shift of activity. Here sky-blue walls sing out against white-paneled concealed storage. The coat rack has a midcentury modern appeal.

Left Stairway to heaven: treads and risers are painted a rich, deep blue, making a graphic contrast to the smooth planes of white walls.

Below left Small spaces, such as bathrooms and cloakrooms, can take big decorative statements, since you will only be using them for limited amounts of time and are less likely to tire of the effect.

Below right A rainbow staircase fully exploits the ability of color to generate surprise and delight.

CONTRAST AND SURPRISE

Color is an excellent way of waking things up a little, particularly in self-contained spaces or circulation areas where we don't linger for long. What might be tiring to live with for extended periods on a daily basis can be supremely energizing in small doses.

Many people play safe with hallways and other connecting spaces in the home, opting for a serviceable, discreet, neutral palette. Yet there are advantages in treating these areas in a bolder fashion. Entryways, lobbies, and landings are all about views—from room to room, from inside to out, from upstairs to down. A jolt of color strikes a positive, inviting note and helps to tie different areas of the home together.

Many entryways are relatively dark places, which call for colors from the warm end of the spectrum. Unless there is top-lighting or a sunny aspect, steer clear of the chillier shades.

Paint is only one way of adding color to hallways. Color underfoot, such as a bright flat-weave stair carpet or runner, can be equally effective. So, too, can a collection of colorful pictures displayed on the walls.

Strong color is equally at home in relatively small, self-contained areas, such as bathrooms. The downstairs bathroom, for example, can be just the place to indulge your fondness for Schiaparelli-pink and give your guests a smile in the process.

ACCENT

Left Books, periodicals, framed pictures, and flowers are all details that have the ability to inject accents of color into the interior. Here the glossy green cabinet provides another focal point within a contemporary space.

Below This collection of ceramic jars and vases has been grouped in color families to make the display more coherent.

Decorative accents are to interiors what accessories are to outfits. Just as a handbag, a pair of shoes, or a vivid necktie can sharpen a whole fashion look and bring it into focus, so, too, can brightly colored details in an interior, such as pillow covers, lamp shades, throws, decorative objects, and pictures. Even something as ephemeral as a vase of flowers can deliver a pop of color that lifts an interior out of the humdrum and makes it sing.

Generally small in scale and often inexpensive, accents have the benefit of not commiting you to a wholesale makeover should you fancy a change. For those who fight a little shy of using strong color more extensively, playing about with accents is also a great way to gain confidence.

Surprising combinations often come from experimentation. The color scheme of the living room in our new London flat is based on soft reds and blues against a plain background, with brighter red accents in the form of pillows and throws. The introduction of a couple of vivid green touches—a bright-green "exploded" lamp base and a greeny-blue dish—added a dash of unexpected vibrancy.

How to use color accents

✻

Where the background is essentially neutral and subdued, almost any strong accent color will be eye-catching.

✻

Don't overdo it. Where every accent is a different color, the effect will be muddled rather than uplifting.

✻

Exploit the power of complementary pairs (see page 23). A small accent of bright orange will leap out of a scheme that is based on shades of blue.

Below left A Damien Hirst spot painting, 'Valium' (2000), and Vintage PEL chairs with green tubular frames introduce subtle dashes of color in an all-white dining room.

Below right Incidental arrangements of flowers provide fresh notes of color that are all the more welcome for their ephemeral nature.

Right The red lips displayed on the Fornasetti plate have color echoes in the glassware arranged on top of the deep-yellow credenza.

FOCAL POINT

Left Green kitchen cabinets provide a focal point of strong color within a space that is otherwise decorated in natural and neutral tones—exposed wooden ceiling, concrete floor, and gray wool upholstery.

Below left A blue mosaic wall makes a feature of a shower enclosure.

Below right In fairly restrained, minimal surroundings, colorful seat upholstery makes a statement of its own.

Whereas accent colors are all about providing little jolts of visual pleasure and leading the eye from place to place, when color is used as a focal point it commands your attention. It's all about scale: a chair seat upholstered in red is a detail; a red upholstered sofa is a statement.

Because you are dealing with a larger surface area, it's generally best to limit yourself to a single focal point per space. Two brightly colored centres of attraction will war with one another and generate a feeling of unease—your eye won't know where to look. Similarly, focal points tend to be most effective when the rest of the decoration is relatively restrained.

Focal points also work best when there is some reason for their existence. For example, a feature wall that indicates a change of activity in an open-plan space has a certain logic to it, but a feature wall that anchors nothing begs a question.

Bear in mind that whichever color you choose to highlight must have sufficient intensity to bear the scrutiny—while pale shades may be very intriguing in certain contexts, they simply don't have sufficient energy to act as foregrounds. As with any other dominant use of color, ultimately, your decision will depend on the orientation of the space and the existing light levels within it, along with the type of atmosphere you are trying to create.

BACKGROUND

Left Yellow is a sunny, upbeat color that needs plenty of natural light to look its best, as in this bright kitchen with its glazed skylight.

Below While the floor occupies a significant proportion of surface area, strong color statements are not as dominant as they would be on walls.

Bottom Red upholstered chairs sing out against moody blue walls. Blue is a naturally recessive shade.

White or off-white walls and pale or neutral-toned floors have become something of a default setting in the contemporary home. The vogue for minimalism in the last decade of the 20th century undoubtedly has had an influence, a trend that harked back even further to the first modernist interiors with their defiant rejection of superficial decoration. However, I think it is fair to say that many people choose plain backgrounds today not out of principle, but out of fear of getting it wrong.

Clearly it does require a certain degree of confidence to use color on a large scale. Walls and floors occupy a considerable amount of surface area, which means that how they are decorated can potentially have an enormous impact on the mood and atmosphere of a room, for good or ill. There is also a tension between what we expect of backgrounds—which is that they provide a discreet setting for daily life—and color—which can't help but call attention to itself.

While strong, intense shades can be a little too domineering in many circumstances, there are many edgy, luminous shades—both at the cool and warm ends of the spectrum—that are well worth experimenting with. The right background color in the right context can be very expressive. In our bedroom in our house in the country, the walls are painted a cheerful, uplifting shade of yellow. It's always a joy to wake up in the morning and see the sun is shining again—if only indoors.

TYPES
OF
COLOR
SCHEMES

Below left A single-color scheme in buttercup yellow is offset with plenty of white.

Below right Shades of blue and blue-green add up to an easy-going harmonious scheme.

There are many different ways of putting colors together in the interior, some riskier than others—from one-note or coordinated compositions to wilder flights of fancy featuring vibrant, electric clashes.

✳

Single-color schemes are pretty well fail-safe, as long as you choose the right color for the context and existing light levels. Offset them with neutral tones or plenty of white. A good example would be a bathroom with deep-blue walls contrasting with white woodwork and porcelain fixtures. Beware of relentless coordination, however, which can be deadening.

✳

Harmonious color schemes combine tones and shades of colors that sit near each other on the artist's color wheel—cool blues, blue-greens, and grays, for example, or warm pinks, oranges, and reds. Neutral and natural schemes work on the same basis—palettes of cream, terra cotta, and various shades of brown, from biscuit to burnt umber.

Below left A single-color scheme in buttercup yellow is offset with plenty of white.

Below right Shades of blue and blue-green add up to an easy-going harmonious scheme.

Below left The jolting contrast of complementary colors, in this case blue and orange, has great vibrancy.

Below centre Graphic schemes featuring dark colors contrasted with white have added impact when patterns are graphic, too.

Below right Most eccentric of all are clashing schemes, particularly those that feature colors such as purple, pink, and magenta.

❈
Complementary schemes need careful handling. Proportion is key: choose one color of a complementary pair to use on a bigger scale and set it off with detail or trim that displays the other—think of a red blanket with a narrow green binding, for example.

❈
Graphic schemes make use of the dynamic pairing of black and white, perhaps with a brighter or primary shade thrown into the mix. This combination works particularly well expressed in geometric designs, such as stripes, spots, and checkerboard effects.

❈
Clashing schemes are not for the faint-hearted. Shocking-pink and purple, turquoise and magenta, and other electric combinations have an aesthetic that is decidedly offbeat.

SURFACE
AND
FINISH

Left While they are all tonally very similar, the blue painted wall, painted stool, and slate flooring reveal their textural differences in the way light is reflected off their surfaces.

Below left Stone cladding used on the walls and bath surround displays a pleasing textural variety that more than compensates for the neutral tones.

Below right Although the color scheme is muted, the textural contrast provided by the leather seating, raftered ceiling, and cotton rug adds depth of interest.

The material character of different surfaces and finishes—their texture, tone, and light-reflecting qualities—naturally will have an impact on the way color is delivered. A black slate floor, for example, will appear subtly different to ebonized floorboards, even before you take in the way the surface appeals to your other senses—how it sounds and how it feels to walk across. When you choose a specific material or finish, you are choosing a whole package, not simply color, but also texture and, to some extent, pattern.

PATINA OF USE

With natural materials, another dimension also comes into play, and that is time. Wood, stone, brick, and leather are just some of the materials that have the potential to age well and to acquire a pleasing patina of use. Tonal shifts—either fading or darkening—along with scratches, scuffs, and other superficial signs of wear add a depth of character that is entirely missing from artificial materials subjected to similar treatment.

TEXTURAL VARIETY

The grain of wood, the riven or honed surface of stone, the nubbly surface of natural weaves, and the smooth sheen of stainless steel all add a dimension of texture to interior decoration that is all the more welcome when colors are muted. Format also contributes a degree of patterning, which increases the vitality of these materials. The rhythm of wooden floorboards, the tight grid of tilework, and the blurred, shimmering effect of mosaic have an inherent dynamism that is very appealing.

Below These fresh, contemporary patterns represent an updated version of Delft tilework.

Right The studded texture of the green rubber flooring is echoed in the tight grid of white mosaic facing the bathtub.

SYNTHETIC MATERIALS

I am not a huge fan of synthetic surfaces and finishes, preferring the integrity of natural materials in most circumstances. They often cost more, but they last better and repay the effort you make to maintain them properly.

Where artificial materials do score highly, however, is in terms of color range. Many synthetics are produced in a huge number of colors and patterns, and, provided you don't compromise on basic practicality, this can be a very persuasive advantage. In general, it's best to avoid synthetic materials that are aping their natural counterparts—"wood-effect" laminate, for example—in favor of cheerful solid-color or abstract or geometric designs.

❈
Composites
Solid materials, such as Corian, can be shaped and worked to make counters and backsplashes.

❈
Linoleum
Strictly speaking a natural product, lino comes in a range of soft, mottled shades and delivers many practical benefits, being nonslip, hypoallergenic, and antibacterial.

❈
Rubber
Whether sheet or tile, rubber flooring is entirely synthetic, these days. The color range offered by some manufacturers is incredibly wide; shades are bright and saturated. One producer guarantees to color-match any Pantone swatch.

❈
Vinyl and laminate
The better grades may be expensive but they are longer-lasting and more convincing. Styles, patterns, and colors vary widely.

❈
Ceramic tile
Again, there is a vast range of colors and designs on the market and a broad range of formats—from large square tiles, to Metro tiles, to mosaic—a factor that alters the aesthetic considerably. Hand-glazed tiles are expensive but particularly luminous.

PAINT PRACTICALITIES

Left This mushroomy taupe makes the perfect backdrop for the abstract painting by Hervé Half.

Below Paint that has a good depth of color always includes a high proportion of good-quality pigment.

One of the quickest and easiest ways to introduce color into your home is with a lick of paint. Walls, woodwork, floors, cabinets, and furniture can all be transformed for relatively little expense and effort—with the additional advantage that you can always paint over them again if you are unhappy with the result.

But there is more to paint formulations than meets the eye. Working with Master Paintmakers, the company that has been our partner in developing the Paint by Conran range, has really brought home to me the importance of quality in paint manufacture.

❉ **Durability** The best paints will withstand knocks and scuffs in high-traffic areas. Marks will be easy to scrub away without lifting the paint surface.

❉ **Coverage** Good paints will cover greater surface areas, meaning you get more for your money. You will also need fewer coats to achieve the right degree of color saturation.

❉ **Depth of color** This is reliant on both the quality and concentration of pigments used in the paint. The better the pigments and the greater the proportion in which they are used, the truer, more intense and more luminous the color will be on the wall.

❉ **Environmental friendliness** Increasingly, the better paint manufacturers are reducing the number of harmful chemicals in their formulations in favour of natural ingredients. This results in paints that have next to no odor and are far better for the environment, both to produce and use. Recyclable packaging makes the products even greener.

❉ **Specific formulations** Kitchen and bathroom paints have antifungal properties that make them resistant to mold.

READY-MADE PALETTES

Left Inspiration for a decorative scheme can come from what might be called "found palettes," such as the colors displayed in a gray painting or rug.

Overleaf The living room in my new London apartment features a storage wall for books and display, including a collection of framed butterflies—one of my passions since boyhood.

MOOD BOARDS

Some people are fortunate to have an innate color sense and know exactly how to translate their ideas into a successful decorative scheme. Most of us, however, need to spend some time learning how to look.

These days, it has never been easier to capture fleeting moments of inspiration—the camera on your cellphone means you need never miss a sight that intrigues you, whether it's a market stall, flowerbed, or store front. With a few clicks, you can upload these images to a visual file on your desktop or share them on social media sites, such as Pinterest or Tumblr. The technology may be unimaginably advanced to those of us who began their creative life in the pencil and paper era, but essentially what you are creating is a mood board, an archive of inspiration to shape your ideas.

Once you start to see some sort of theme emerging, a preference for a particular family of colors, for example, the next stage is to shift from the virtual to the real. Gather together samples and swatches and play around with them to assess how they work together.

✲ Experiment with proportion. If you are thinking about using a vivid shade as an accent, that sample or swatch should be proportionately smaller on your mood board.
✲ The bigger the sample or swatch, the easier it will be to assess its effect.
✲ Paint test-patches of color in different areas of the room to judge the impact of varying light levels. Certain colors "mount up" or appear more intense in larger doses than they do on colorcards, so the bigger the test-patch, the more accurate your assessment will be.
✲ Colors will look different under artificial light than they do in the day.

DESIGNERS' PALETTES

If you haven't got the time or the inclination to explore your color preferences via mood boards, there is nothing wrong with taking a short cut. Ready-made color palettes offer the opportunity to benefit from the expertise of designers, stylists, and other professionals who work with color every day.

When we were putting together our Paint by Conran range, we consulted a color psychologist. After a great deal of thought, we had already chosen nearly a hundred colors, all inspired by British plants and landscapes. Her role was to edit our selection into five distinct collections of colors that naturally work well together—and even, in one instance, to identify a shade of blue that was missing.

✲ Specialized or heritage paint suppliers often have ranges designed to evoke a particular period or style, if you are after a retro or historical look. The same is true of reference books or on-line sites focusing on the décor of a specific era.

✲ Inspiration can start at home, with something you already own— for example, a patterned rug, fabric, or picture. Picking out the various colors in the design to use as backgrounds, focal points, or accents will guarantee a harmonious result.

✲ Other sources of ready-made palettes include features in interior magazines or on blogposts— all the better if they detail sources and stockists.

PART TWO **COLOR BY COLOR**

blue

blue

The color of the sea, sky, and distant hills, blue is inherently airy, spacious, and contemplative. It's my favorite color, and I am not alone. Surveys show that almost half the people in the West say the same. We certainly wear a lot of it—blue denim, in particular, but also various uniforms, from *bleu de travail* and business suits to navy and air-force blue.

Blue corresponds to the shorter wavelengths of light. Because these shorter wavelengths are scattered more readily by atmospheric gases, the sky and the distant horizon appear blue. Similarly, the sea looks blue, partly because it reflects the sky, but also because the longer wavelengths of light are absorbed in great depths of water.

All colors have their contradictory associations, but blue perhaps more than others. Blue is both sacred and profane, uplifting and gloomy. The transcendent color of divinity, spirituality, and heaven, it also evokes the decidedly off-color—"blue movies" and "blue jokes," as well as melancholy and depression.

TRUE BLUE

Blue is so prevalent, these days, that it can be hard to appreciate just how expensive and rare the color once was. Aside from plant-based dyes, such as indigo and woad, the earliest true blue was made from lapis lazuli, a semi-precious mineral mined in Afghanistan and exported all over the world. The pigment was so valuable that artists' contracts often stipulated their patrons would bear the cost of supplying it.

SHADES
OF
BLUE

Left This powerful decorative scheme is based around several shades of deep blue, from indigo to ultramarine to cobalt.

Blue encompasses a wide range of shades and tones, from the lightest ice-blue to the deepest indigo. This makes it a hugely versatile color in decoration, whether it is used as a background or forms part of a pattern.

Bluish white
An icy tone that works well as a space-enhancing background where light levels are high.

Powder blue
Combine pastel blue with grays and edgier blues for elegance, or orange and brown for a midcentury palette.

French blue
Soft, warm and easy on the eye, this grayed blue has an appealing countrified look.

Sky blue
Sky blues, such as cerulean and azure, are supremely optimistic and work well with most other colors.

Greenish blue
Turquoise, aquamarine, duck-egg, and teal are edgy shades that vary in appearance as light levels change.

Cobalt
A strong, cool shade, cobalt is the blue of classic Chinese blue-and-white porcelain.

Prussian blue
The first synthetic blue, developed in the early 18th century, this color is dark and atmospheric.

Ultramarine
An intense blue with a slight violet tinge, ultramarine was historically highly prized.

Navy
Sober and elegant, navy is a good substitute for black as a defining contrast in graphic schemes.

Indigo
A deep, purplish blue, often found in naturally dyed ethnic textiles, indigo is very susceptible to fading.

BLUE
BACKGROUNDS

Left Greenish blue is a particularly expressive shade. Here it strikes an elegant note of peaceful repose as a backdrop to a bedroom.

Below Blue mosaic is deservedly a popular choice for bathroom décor. The texture of the tilework adds vivacity to the cool, watery color.

Both expansive and restful, blue works well as a background color. The right shade in the right context can be fresh, revitalizing, and space-enhancing. Get it wrong, however, and the effect can be draining and downright inhospitable.

LIGHT LEVELS

Blue is a cool, distancing color. In rooms that receive a lot of natural light, particularly those with a southerly or westerly aspect, blue backgrounds—especially those that are lighter in tone—will enhance the sense of space and generate an overall feeling of brightness and airiness. Where light levels are lower or cooler, however, the same shade of blue may be uncomfortably chilly and a little depressing. In these darker areas, the answer is not necessarily to avoid using blue as a background color altogether, but to opt for deeper, more saturated shades that are moody and expressive. At Barton Court, my house in the country, I've painted a hallway deep blue to go with my prized collection of Bugatti-blue pedal cars that hang along the length of one wall.

BLUE BATHROOMS

The obvious association of blue with the sea—and water in general—means that blue is often a very successful color when used for bathroom decoration. Most bathrooms tend to be on the small side compared with living areas and are usually self-contained spaces, which means you can afford to be more daring in your choice of background color— intense shades of ultramarine, turquoise, and aquamarine evoke a suitably watery theme. Blue mosaic is particularly effective, with its shimmering effect that is reminiscent of light dancing on water.

BLUE
AND
WHITE

Below Moorish tiling on the floor and up to chair rail height on the wall displays a variant on the blue-and-white theme.

Bottom Blue-and-white china is homely and domesticated. In Soup Kitchen, the café I opened in the 1950s, we sold soup in Cornishware bowls for one shilling a serving.

Pretty much as fail-safe a combination as there can be, blue and white is the classic domestic pairing. White lends a graphic crispness to the airiness and distancing effect of blue, with the overall scheme being simple, fresh, and charming.

Embedded in this combination are associations that reflect a long history of its use in the interior—think of Delft tiles, Chinese blue-and-white 'Willow' pattern porcelain, or the comforting appeal of Cornishware crockery. Blue was once believed to be a repellent for flies, hence its widespread appearance in the whitewashed kitchens of former times.

Another obvious reference point is the sea. Blue-and-white striped fabrics have a jaunty nautical look, evoking striped Breton fishermen's tops, sailor's uniforms, and white-crested waves.

The proportion in which the colors are used will have a greater impact on the overall effect than the precise shades involved. A deep-blue wall set off with gleaming white woodwork, for example, will read differently from a white fabric with narrow blue stripes or spots. But even where patterning is more figurative, the combination retains a keen graphic edge.

Cornishware
✻

There are few sights more evocative of the traditional farmhouse kitchen than a hutch displaying a cheery collection of Cornishware bowls, pitchers, mugs, and plates. The crockery, with its distinctive blue-and-white banding, was first produced in the 1920s using a lathe to strip away bands of blue slip to reveal the underlying white clay.

This page Blue and white makes a simple and fresh combination for a country kitchen. The robust kitchen cabinet doors are made of painted planked wood.

MOODY BLUES

Left A soft blue-gray wall has a cool, distancing effect. The scrubbed-wood table and wooden chairs are similarly reticent.

Below A deep-blue backsplash provides a strong color accent to contrast with the seamless white kitchen cabinetry.

Blue-violet, blue-gray, and blue-green—shades of blue that contain elements of their neighbors on the color wheel—have an appealing ambiguity that is most evident in the way that they appear to shift in tone as the light conditions vary throughout the day. Luminous and full of vitality, pale shades of these moody blues work well as backgrounds. Deeper, more saturated versions make excellent contrasts and accents.

BLUE-VIOLET

An elegant shade of blue, particularly in its lighter tones, blue-violet is a useful background color in rooms where natural light levels are less than ideal. The warm violet tinge tempers blue's natural tendency to chilliness while preserving its space-enhancing qualities.

BLUE-GRAY

Elegant shades of blue-gray were a classic feature of 18th-century décor, when the emphasis was on creating light-filled interiors and enhancing the sense of space. The Swedish version was Gustavian gray, but similar shades crop up in Georgian and Colonial color schemes. In the contemporary home, where space and light are also prized, this color is equally effective as a background. It also makes a good reticent finish for flooring, woodwork, and wood paneling.

BLUE-GREEN

At their most intense, the blue-green colors of aquamarine and turquoise evoke seaside locations around the world, from Martha's Vineyard to the Caribbean, where they often crop up both in interiors and as exterior trim and accent. As befits a shade that straddles two colors, blue-green combines the best of both, making a bold yet soothing backdrop.

Tiffany & Co.
✳

Light versions of blue-green, such as duck- or robin's-egg blue, have overtones of luxury and sophistication, as epitomized by the trademarked signature color of Tiffany & Co. packaging.

NATURAL BLUES

Below A dusky shade of blue makes a relaxing background for a bedroom. Natural blues are soft and easy on the eye.

Right Walls the color of well-worn, washed-out jeans are teamed with linen sofa and chair upholstery and an indigo cotton rug.

Plants, such as indigo and woad, have been employed for thousands of years to make the color blue. Woad was the most common source of blue dye for clothing and textiles in Europe until indigo began to be imported from India during the 15th century.

Much later, after indigo had itself been superseded by synthetic pigments, William Morris experimented with natural dyes at his printworks at Merton Abbey Mills, south London. Indigo only fixes on oxidation, and a favorite spectacle for visitors was the sight of sea-green skeins of yarn being lifted from the vat of indigo dye, only to turn deep blue after a few minutes' exposure to air.

Indigo was the natural dye used to color the first denim jeans—"denim" is a corruption of "de Nîmes," Nîmes being the city in France where the cloth was first manufactured, while "jeans" refers to Genoa in Italy (Gênes in French), where the first denim trousers were sold. Today, these soft, dusky blues are as easy to live with as they are to wear. Blue, incidentally, is the color most prone to fading—so the vogue for washed-out denim makes a fashion out of an inevitability.

How to use natural blues

✻
As upholstery
Indigo, like all deep blues, makes a good choice for sofa upholstery. The dark shade minimizes the bulk of large items of furniture.

✻
As soft furnishings
Natural blues crop up in many ethnic textiles, such as hand-printed Indian cottons, ikat, and batik.

✻
As flooring & cladding
Slate is the material that most closely approximates indigo in color—slate-blue floors, tiling, and cladding make atmospheric backdrops.

BLUE ACCENTS

Left The use of blue as an accent or feature wall is enhanced here by the crisp white seating, white tiling, and striking geometric tiled floor.

Below left Kingfisher blue, bright and arresting, emphasizes the clean, boxy lines of a modern sofa.

Below right Kitchen cabinets and built-in storage in a strong blue make a vivid statement in a kitchen featuring a robust use of metal, wood, and stone.

You may think that a cool, distancing color such as blue does not naturally lend itself to use as an accent. While it is true that most blues work better in the background, you only have to catch a fleeting glimpse of a kingfisher by the water's edge or a jay flitting from tree to tree to appreciate that blue, too, can be eye-catching.

Needless to say, the precise shade of blue is all-important. No one is ever going to make an effective accent out of navy. What's wanted, instead, are those electric blues, such as ultramarine, cerulean, and turquoise, which are so vivid that they suggest the synthetic. The ultimate blue accents are neon and fluorescent blue.

Blue that is backlit will naturally attract more attention. A collection of bright-blue glass vases and bowls on a sunny windowsill makes an effective display, as do blue glass transoms or panels in doors, while translucent blue panels lit from behind create glowing focal points in built-in areas, such as kitchens and bathrooms.

Blue accents are also more effective when they don't have much competition from other colors. Blue is inevitably going to stand out when the rest of the scheme is based around natural or neutral shades—think of an armchair upholstered in sky blue in a room where the walls are white and the floor is pale wood.

BLUE
SCHEMES

Left A number of shades of soft blue-gray work effortlessly together, with the orange discs in the pendant light adding a splash of complementary verve.

Below left A stronger version of the same color combination partners the shelving's orange backdrop with a deep-blue rug.

Bottom left Dulled-down blues and blue-grays, with a touch of ocher in the wallpaper pattern, make a soothing and restful scheme for a bedroom.

Blue comes in so many different shades and goes so well with so many colors that it is relatively easy to come up with a successful decorative scheme. Blue clashes with nothing. Its calming presence can reconcile colors that would otherwise not go together—like a little patch of blue sky that lifts the spirits. For example, a surprisingly good combination is blue with brown, a smart pairing that has retro overtones.

HARMONIOUS

The old saying "blue and green should never be seen" could not be further from the truth. The portion of the spectrum from green to blue to violet contains shades that harmonize with each other effortlessly. Add tonal variations to the mix, and the result becomes quite subtle. An obvious reference point is found in nature—blue sky and green fields—but the edgier shades of petrol blue, turquoise, and a pale lilac in combination can suggest more exotic settings, from North Africa to the Caribbean.

Previous pages Blue and green—with a dash of yellow—is a surprisingly effective combination.

Below The smallest touches of a complementary color can bring a room to life. Here yellow pillows sing out against blue painted louvered shutters.

Right When pairing complementary colors, think about the proportion of each shade, along with the tone. In this living room, a balanced combination of yellow and blue is offset with plenty of neutrals to calm things down.

COMPLEMENTARY

Depending on the color model to which you subscribe, blue's complementary color is either orange or yellow.
In tandem with blue, both can form the basis of electric, vitalizing schemes.

Blue and yellow—or blue and gold—is a combination that has many natural counterparts, along with associations that go far back in time—as the celestial pairing that crops up on the pages of medieval illuminated manuscripts, for example, or on the coat of arms of the kings of France. Mixed together, blue and yellow make green, and it is this striving for a central balance and harmony that gives the combination its stability and power.

Blue and orange has a crisper, more contemporary feel. As with any combination that is based on the inherent energy of complementaries, getting the proportion of each shade right is important. So, too, is tone. The more successful schemes feature colors that are tonally very similar.

GRAPHIC

Spots, stripes, and plaids featuring blue with white, black, and gray are geometric designs that combine freshness with a pleasing sense of rhythm. Because these patterns share a basic affinity, you can vary the scale of the repeats and even the type of design in the same interior without risk of overkill.

More forthright—and requiring much more careful handling—are schemes that feature the primary colors of blue, red, and yellow in their clearest, least adulterated form. The intensity of the bold combination requires an element of tight control, in the form of Mondrian-like compositions of colored planes.

DEEP PURPLE

Left Dark-purple chiffon curtains filter the light, creating a mood of sophistication and theatricality in this bedroom.

Below It takes confidence to employ the dark, bruised shades of plum and eggplant a on a large scale.

A mixture of blue and red, purple is a bruised, brooding color that can be rich and sumptuous or downright difficult, depending on how you handle it. Once the exclusive preserve of royalty and the priesthood, there remains something a little over-the-top about the color.

❖ The lighter tones of violet, lilac, and lavender are undoubtedly the most versatile. Pale lavender, like blue-gray, makes a lustrous background that seems to trap the light.

❖ Darker purples—such as plum, eggplant, and heathery, tweedy shades—are moodier, especially in large doses. In the right context, these colors make sophisticated backdrops, but they are easier to control in the form of soft furnishings—as the prevalent colors of upholstery, blankets, and throws, for instance.

❖ The combination of purple, light blue, and brown has a retro appeal and often crops up on vintage textiles.

Purple
❖

Since ancient times, purple has been associated with high status and privilege. Tyrian purple, a dye used to color the togas of Roman emperors, was extracted from the glands of sea snails in an expensive and laborious process; sumptuary laws through the ages guaranteed its exclusivity, occasionally on pain of death.

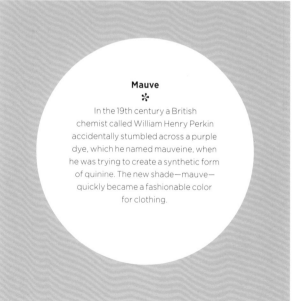

Mauve
❖

In the 19th century a British chemist called William Henry Perkin accidentally stumbled across a purple dye, which he named mauveine, when he was trying to create a synthetic form of quinine. The new shade—mauve—quickly became a fashionable color for clothing.

CLASSIC
CONRAN
COLOR
ULTRAMARINE

When devising decorative schemes, interior designers often take cues from the colors that feature most prominently in their clients' wardrobes. Anyone taking a peek in mine would see a lot of blue, specifically the strong, deep blue of my cotton shirts. I have been wearing this particular color for years. The shirts are made by the classic British clothier Turnbull & Asser; sadly, this precise shade has recently been discontinued, so it's a good job I don't mind wearing things that are a bit worn and frayed.

One of the reasons I like this color so much is that its intensity brings to mind Yves Klein Blue (or International Klein Blue, as it was officially patented in 1961). The French artist Yves Klein began exhibiting single-color canvases or monochromes in the 1950s. By 1957 he had focused solely on one color: ultramarine. The color itself was the art. Later, and somewhat notoriously, he used the color in performance art. Nude models, painted in Yves Klein Blue, rolled around on canvases, essentially being used as "living brushes."

Another association—also French—is the color of the traditional *bleu de travail*: a simple, robust cotton jacket with practical pockets. Once a common sight piled high on market stalls all over the country, *bleu de travail* was typically worn by laborers and manual workers. Nowadays you are more likely to find vintage versions on the backs of those involved in the creative industries.

orange

Left Orange strikes a positive, cheerful note in this contemporary kitchen with its pale wood cabinets. The color of the chairs is echoed by a similar shade featured in the scatter rug and enameled kettle.

orange

Orange has all the attention-seeking qualities of red, with the uplifting cheerfulness of yellow—hardly surprising since it is a blend of the two. It has long been a significant color in Asian religions, most notably Buddhism. In the West, it has strong associations with Protestantism.

Orange is a color of high visibility. Like red, it is a warm, advancing shade that puts us on alert. Sale signs, lifeboats, buoyancy jackets, and amber warning lights all make use of orange's natural tendency to jump out at us. In nature, too, orange sounds a note of caution, particularly in combination with black—think of the banding on a tiger or a wasp. Orange is also said to be the first color that babies learn to distinguish.

Other natural associations are with the fruit from which it takes its name. Oranges, like many other fruits and vegetables—such as peaches, apricots, mangoes, pumpkins, gourds, carrots, squash, and various types of melon—contain carotene, a pigment involved in photosynthesis. Darker versions of the color include the mellow, earthy shades of terra cotta and brick.

Warm and spicy, optimistic and easy-going, orange has a fresh, contemporary quality that derives in part from its prevalence in midcentury modern decorative schemes. Further back, orange was also a key shade in Art Deco palettes, which were themselves inspired by the bold, striking scenery and costumes of the Ballets Russes.

TANGERINE

The brightest and clearest shades of orange make natural color accents, adding a touch of zest to a scheme. Upbeat, jolly and a little quirky, tangerine has a fresh, modern appeal that always strikes a cheerful note. The smallest touch of bright orange—whether in the form of a pillow, light shade, throw, or vase—will always make its presence felt. Tangerine brings a certain energy to a space, making it suitable for rooms where a certain degree of stimulation is welcome, such as kitchens, living rooms, and studies.

How to use tangerine

✳

Lighting
Bright orange fabric or parchment shades create a cozy, intimate light.

✳

Enameled accessories
Displays of everyday kitchen equipment can be enlivened with tangerine-colored enameled pots, pans, and casseroles. The classic Le Creuset casserole, for example, is a bright flame-orange.

✳

Upholstery and soft furnishings
Although it is definitely attention-seeking, tangerine works surprisingly well as upholstery—even on large pieces such as sofas, provided the designs are clean-lined. It also injects a welcome dose of liveliness when used to cover armchairs and chair seats. Bright-orange rugs, pillows, and throws make other good accents.

✳

Decorative display
Tangerine was a popular color in the 1930s and often appears—with blues and greens—in the ceramics of the period. The designs of Clarice Cliff and the patterns of Shelley pottery typically display a great deal of the color.

TERRA COTTA

Left A live-work space features a wall of exposed brickwork, its charming irregularity supplying a characterful reminder of the building's history.

Below Exposed and sealed brick makes a warm backdrop to a modern kitchen, the liveliness of its surface texture providing an effective contrast to the smooth finishes of the cabinets, counters. and appliances.

The more muted, earthier tones of orange make excellent backgrounds, especially when expressed in material form rather than as applied decoration. The warmth of these shades generates a feeling of coziness without being overly insistent, and the textural quality adds a great sense of character to a space.

BRICK

Walls of exposed brick are the height of fashion in cafés, bars, and restaurants in hip urban areas, where they usually go hand in hand with the trend for authentic, handcrafted, and artisanal accessories and produce. The same back-to-basics honesty can be very appealing in the interior.

It is important not to overdo it, however. One wall of exposed brick—or at most two—is enough. More than that and the raw, unfinished quality of the surfaces might begin to seem a little brutal.

The effect produced will be very different depending on whether the brickwork is old or new. Old brickwork, stripped of its applied finishes, has a rugged, characterful appearance and can be surprisingly variegated in tone and texture. In lofts and other converted spaces, such surfaces provide a welcome reminder of the building's working past. New brickwork, particularly if it is composed of engineered brick, has a sleeker, more homogenous look. Here the association is with midcentury design: bare brick walls make a natural counterpart to Scandinavian modern furniture and hardwood flooring.

Below left The walls of this bathroom are finished in polished plasterwork in a rich burnt orange, a traditional finish of Moroccan riads.

Below right Machine-made terra cotta quarry tiles have a clean, contemporary appeal and are highly suitable for use with underfloor heating.

Right Hexagonal floor tiles in a burnished terra cotta make a lustrous floor. At night, the interlocking daisy shapes of the PS Maskros pendant light, by Ikea, create patterns on the ceiling and walls of this bedroom.

PLASTER

Exposed pinky-gray plasterwork has a similar mellow quality to exposed brick, although it lacks a degree of textural depth. The earth tones can be brought out with polishing and waxing.

Tadelakt, the Moroccan version of polished plasterwork, typically has a deep burnt-orange color. A traditional finish for the walls of riads, it has a beautifully mottled surface.

Dusting
✳

Both exposed brick and plaster have a tendency to "dust" without any further treatment. A light, transparent seal applied to the wall will keep the surface intact without affecting the color or texture. Sealing or waxing will also provide protection from water staining and grease marks, which can otherwise be a problem with raw plaster.

TERRA COTTA FLOORING

Earth-based materials, such as terra cotta tiles, quarry tiles and brick, are very effective as floors. Like stone, these materials have good thermal mass, which means they warm up slowly and release heat slowly. This make them an ideal choice for use in homes designed to exploit passive solar strategies, or in combination with underfloor heating. Visually, this earthy shade of orange is less dominant when used underfoot than when it is used as a background color on walls, but the nature of these materials means that they inevitably suggest a countrified aesthetic.

MID-CENTURY MODERN

Left Orla Kiely is famous for her love of midcentury modern design, the inspiration behind her hugely successful fashion and homewares collections. Her London kitchen displays her signature style—and is very reminiscent of my old kitchen in London back in the 1950s.

Below Candy-striped fabric has been used to upholster this classic vintage sofa, the Ercol Studio Couch. The design, first released in the late 1950s, has recently proved to be so popular on auction sites such as eBay that the company has reissued it.

Various shades of orange, from tangy tangerine to rich burnt orange, are common features of midcentury modern palettes. The color also played a big role in Scandinavian modern design in the 1940s and 1950s, and continued to strike a positive, slightly irreverent note in color schemes inspired by Pop Art and psychedelia right up to the 1970s. What was once defiantly modern has, 40 years on, acquired a nostalgic retro tinge.

ORANGE AND TEAK

Much Scandinavian modern furniture was produced in teak, an extremely stable hardwood with a warm orange-brown color. Today teak is an endangered wood, but original pieces remain widely collected—and now come with increasingly high price tags. Orange upholstery complements teak-framed furniture, especially bench seating. Bright orange also draws attention to sleek, organic forms, such as those of classic chairs designed by Verner Panton, Eero Saarinen, and Hans Wegner.

ORANGE AND OLIVE

This classic midcentury pairing can be given further depth and interest with the addition of brown and a light, dulled blue. A wallpaper featuring some or all of these colors can be used to create a feature wall, although furnishing fabrics might be easier to live with on a daily basis.

ORANGE AND PURPLE

Bright orange and deep purple make an exceptionally vibrant combination, best mediated with plenty of breathing space. Dulled down, however, so that the orange is a mellow pumpkin color and the purple is closer to a berry shade, and you have a more workable autumnal palette.

CLASHING SCHEMES

Left One way of controlling the wild energy of clashing schemes based on orange, red, and pink is to feature the colors in a geometric, striped, or banded design, such as this vibrant rug.

Below Another possibility is to feature bright, clashing shades as accent colors, with plenty of neutral breathing space.

Partnering orange with red and pink, shades that lie close to it on the color wheel, requires a degree of confidence and careful handling. All clashing schemes, which have their basis in such jarring contrasts, have high levels of energy and *joie de vivre*. Such bright combinations are common in nature—as can been seen in many gardens and florists' shops. They are also a feature of cultures where color is used with great exuberance and lack of inhibition. The pinks, reds, and oranges of Rajasthani saris, for example, betray a love of color that goes well beyond the strictures of the rule book.

How to use orange, red, and pink

✳

Color blocking
Take a leaf out of fashion's book and set planes of these colors next to each other in simple bands or blocks. An example might be a fabric striped in shades of orange, red, and pink, with the geometry of the design exerting a degree of control.

✳

Small-scale patterning
Clashing colors can be somewhat tamed without losing the vibrancy of the combination when you use them on a small scale. Examples include fabric or wallpaper patterned in small repeats, checked and plaid fabrics, such as Madras, or mosaic that similarly combines the colors. Up close, the vitality is there; at a distance, the effect is softer.

✳

Varying scale
Use red and pink as accent colors against a more extensive orange background—for example, as throws or pillows on an upholstered chair or sofa.

COPPER
AND
BRONZE

Left Tom Dixon's Copper pendant light is a modern classic. Here it lends warmth and intimacy to a dining table.

Below Copper cladding makes a rich, lustrous, and light-reflective surface. Be prepared to spend a little time on its maintenance to keep it looking good.

Overleaf, left The PH 3½–3 Copper pendant light was designed in 1929, one of the earliest products in the famous PH series designed by Poul Henningsen.

Overleaf, right Copper's antibacterial qualities make it an excellent choice for a wall cladding or countertop in a kitchen.

Metallic surfaces and finishes made of copper and bronze represent orange in its warmest, shiniest form. In the past, copper featured most often in the interior in the form of beaten fire hoods, doorknobs, drawer pulls, and similar detailing. Today, copper is used with a more modern flair.

❋
Batterie de cuisine
Copper-bottomed pots and pans—the treasured equipment of serious cooks—make a gleaming sculptural display when suspended from hooks.

❋
Pendants and shades
Tom Dixon's Copper Light is a large, pendant, polycarbonate globe, the interior of which is sprayed with a very thin layer of the metal, making a highly reflective shade with a warm glow.

❋
Cladding
Copper wall tiles transform a chimney breast into a glowing focal point, while copper and bronze mosaic tiling makes a lively surface in kitchens, bathrooms, and shower enclosures.

❋
Surfaces
Copper is antibacterial and can be used as a kitchen counter or to face the doors of kitchen cabinets.

❋
Bathroom fittings
Copper is an excellent conductor of heat and a traditional form of cladding for freestanding bathtubs. Contemporary copper sinks are also available.

❋
Spit and polish
Metallic surfaces and finishes require a little upkeep to remain looking their best, and copper is no exception. An alternative to proprietary polish is to rub half a lemon in salt and use this to bring up the luster.

CLASSIC
CONRAN
COLOR
BURNT ORANGE

Warm, mellow, and cheerful, burnt orange is a color very much associated with the fall and harvest time—from the bright shades of turning leaves to ripe gourds and pumpkins in the vegetable garden. Our vegetable garden at our home in the country is not only a plentiful source of fresh food for the table, but also a feast for the eyes and a great source of color inspiration.

Orange fruit and vegetables contain carotene, a pigment named after carrots. Carotene is involved in photosynthesis, transmitting the light energy it absorbs to chlorophyll. When chillier temperatures prevent chlorophyll from reaching the leaves of a tree, they turn various bright shades, from yellow to orange to red, depending on the species of tree

and the suddenness of the cold snap. Japanese maples put on a particularly vivid show during the autumn months.

Burnt orange, less acidic than the citrus shade, is a color that is very easy to live with. From the 1930s onwards, when it was a feature of Art Deco, it has been used in large doses in decorative schemes. The color also has strong associations with midcentury or Scandinavian modern interiors, often cropping up in the patterned wallpaper, textiles, and upholstery of the period, where it combines well with teak, the wood most commonly used to make furniture. I particularly enjoy it as an accent color—either in a display of fruit and vegetables piled on a kitchen platter, or in the form of incidental objects such as glazed vases and pots.

green

green

Balanced, restful, and soothing, green's correspondence with the middle of the visible spectrum means that our eyes have to make little adjustment to see it. In nature it is everywhere and in every conceivable shade and tone, from the deep forest green of fir trees to the light fresh green of new buds. The word "green" itself derives from a linguistic root meaning "grass" or "grow."

Green's natural association with fertility and rebirth could not be more obvious, hence its adoption by environmental parties and associations as part of their identities. But it has negative connotations, too: with envy, illness, poison, and inexperience.

In the interior, green's calming effect and its ability to combine well with numerous other colors make it a key element of many schemes. But you don't have to decorate with green to enjoy it at first hand—any area of the home that opens directly onto a lawn or backyard, or that features expanses of glazing overlooking it, will borrow the color from surrounding planting.

WHY GRASS IS GREEN
The most common natural pigment is chlorophyll, which allows plants to convert sunlight into energy via photosynthesis. Grass and leaves appear green because chlorophyll absorbs both the long and short wavelengths of light—red and blue, respectively.

A SIGHT FOR SORE EYES
It has long been believed that green is a healing, beneficial color for strained eyes. Library lights with green glass shades, green Holland blinds, green awnings, green visors, and tinted glasses are all traditional means of protecting eyes from strong light.

BRITISH RACING GREEN
Racing Green, a deep shade of forest green, was the color adopted by British teams participating in international motor racing during the early to mid-20th century. Since then, it has been a popular color for sports cars.

CITRUS

Below Strong color can be tricky to handle in large doses. Rather than forego it entirely and miss out on the energy it brings to the interior, experiment with displays and other accents. These zesty citrus shades naturally work well together.

Right Green, which is so common a color in nature, is a great way of bringing the indoors closer to the outdoors. Here punchy lime-green kitchen cabinets harmoniously combine with a stunning view of a forested hillside. The pale-blue integrated countertop makes an edgy contrast.

Grass green and leaf green are anchoring colors and can be a little too restful and soporific if they are unmediated by livelier contrasts. The same is not true of the sharp citrus shade of lime, the electric greeny yellow of rapeseed fields, or the fresh greens associated with new spring foliage, rather than the dense canopies of high summer. These vibrant shades are powerful and invigorating—at their brightest, they are almost fluorescent. Their vitality has a strong contemporary appeal.

How to use citrus green

Good combinations

✻
Focal points
Use citrus-greens for stand-alone focal points, to define a feature wall, mark out a spatial divider or for built-in cabinetry.

✻
Citrus shades are an excellent way of adding punch to a decorative scheme that features other softer and more muted greens.

✻
Accents
Lime-green was a popular midcentury modern color; it also crops up in Art Deco palettes. Pillow covers, upholstery, and displays can all be vehicles for introducing bright notes.

✻
In small doses, lime works well with other citrus colors, such as lemon and orange. Lemon, lime, and white is a particularly fresh, airy, and optimistic color combination.

✻
Quality of light
These colors, like yellow, work best in sunny locations, where the warmth of the light emphasizes their vitality. In darker areas, they can look a little sickly.

✻
Lime makes an excellent contrasting— even clashing—color in schemes that feature a lot of deep blue.

THE GREEN ROOM

Left Green is thought to ease eyestrain, which is why it was often the color used to decorate libraries and studies. Here it is used in a saturated way in a contemporary work space-cum-pod that adjoins an open-plan living area.

Below A view of the green "pod" from the main living space. A large skylight bathes the interior in natural light.

All shades of green naturally work well together. Just as a garden or planting plan that relies chiefly on the subtle variations of leaf color will never be dull or discordant, you can't go far wrong basing an interior scheme on these harmonious shades.

GREEN BACKGROUNDS

Until the arrival of synthetic dyes and pigments in the 19th century, bright green was a very difficult shade to reproduce. It was also expensive, which gave it a cachet among the wealthy and privileged. Bright-green rooms set off with crisp white moldings were extremely fashionable in Colonial society.

By the 19th century, darker, more somber colors were popular in decoration. Dark green was a traditional choice for libraries and studies—perhaps because it was believed to ease eyestrain or because its contemplative quality seemed to suit rooms where the focus is inward.

With the exception of citrus greens and some of the edgier greeny blues, green is not a color that is going to set the heart racing. Large doses of green tend to work best in rooms where you are looking to create an atmosphere of peace and tranquillity, such as bedrooms and bathrooms.

QUALITY OF LIGHT

One of the key factors to consider is quality of light. Cool, restful shades of pale leaf green, eau de nil, and celadon make elegant, refined backgrounds in rooms that receive direct sunlight. They also work well in east-facing areas, where the light has a bluish tinge. In darker areas, the same tones can have a slightly bilious look, like the color cast of fluorescent lamps. The moodier, more evocative shades of olive, jade, and pistachio, complex colors that contain elements of warmer or cooler shades, have a contemporary edge and suit a broader range of locations.

Below Green and white is a fresh and airy combination. These graphic patterned tiles have a contemporary edge due to the scale of the repeat.

Bottom Greeny-blue built-in storage units create a restful, contemplative mood in a bathroom.

Right Olive is a classic midcentury modern shade. Here it forms an evocative backdrop to a collection of vintage bowls, pots, and plates.

Overleaf Shades of green, from emerald to greeny gray, offset with plenty of white, generate a feeling of calm repose.

Surfaces and finishes

Blue-green and greeny-gray paint finishes give woodwork, built-in cabinetry, and wooden paneling a certain rustic or countrified quality.

In bathrooms, tongue-and-groove boarding painted a light greeny gray, or ceramic tiles in the same color, make evocative and practical surface treatments.

Thick, toughened glass used to make kitchen counters has a greenish tinge that can be accentuated by lighting.

Fabric in solid shades of green can be a little self-effacing. The textural interest provided by nubblier weaves adds character, especially to upholstery materials; deep-green leather on sofas and chairs has clubby associations and only improves with time and wear.

GREEN
AND
WHITE

Left The crispness of white painted woodwork provides a fresh contrast to a hall decorated in a delicate shade of green. This combination was popular in 18th-century interiors on both sides of the Atlantic.

Below Zigzag tiling reminiscent of Missoni's characteristic textile patterns makes a feature of a kitchen backsplash.

Just as a color will appear much more intense alongside its complementary hue, combining any shade with white gives a feeling of freshness and airiness. In the case of green, the effect is of dappled light through trees or the optimism of new spring growth.

FIGURATIVE DESIGNS

Green's role as a visual anchor in nature finds an echo in many wallpaper and fabric designs, both traditional and contemporary. A classic historic example—albeit one that is still in production today—is William Morris's "Willow" pattern, an ethereal leafy design for both wallpaper and fabric. Stylized leaf and geometric designs are more at home in the contemporary interior.

GEOMETRICS

Spots, stripes, checks, and other geometric patterns have a cheerful informality that suits kitchens, breakfast rooms, family areas and other spaces that see a good deal of daytime use.

Green pigments
✽

Before the advent of synthetic pigments, a process of discovery that began in the 18th century, green was achieved in a number of ways. One common means, which dates back to antiquity, was to mix blue and yellow pigments together. Green earth pigment (terre-verte) was also found in certain clay deposits colored by other minerals. Another method was to scrape off the verdigris that forms on copper, bronze or brass—the resulting blue-green was unstable and highly toxic.

OUTDOORS IN

Left A planter inset into a storage unit serves as a spatial divider and a reminder of the great outdoors. Like any display, indoor plants are much more effective when they are grouped together than when they are dotted about.

Below left A large square window frames a view of a luxuriant tropical garden—a beautiful sight to feast your eyes upon when enjoying a relaxing soak in the bath.

Below right A full-scale photographic mural of lush, leafy woodland serves as a contemporary version of trompe l'oeil.

Blurring the boundaries between indoor and outdoor spaces means you don't have to decorate your interior with green in order to live with it—you need only borrow it. Even the smallest, most minimal gardens—a windowbox on a south-facing sill or a few planters on a balcony, for example—feature at least some green. Most gardens contain a good deal more, in the form of grass and leafy trees and shrubbery.

❊
Make the most of indoor-outdoor connections by extending glazing across the full breadth of a back wall and installing sliding glass doors. Glazed additions, either to the rear or side of the house, also open up the interior to garden views.

❊
Tie indoor and outdoor spaces together by running the same flooring, or flooring of a similar tone, out into the garden in the form of a terraced area. Pale limestone or dark slate, for example, work equally well in both locations, both practically and visually. The connection is further enhanced if the flooring indoors and out is on the same level.

❊
The ultimate green room is the conservatory or sunroom, a place to grow tender plants in a protected setting. Avoid reproduction styles and opt for clean modern lines. I've got a special affection for our sunroom in the country—it's one of my favorite places to sit and sketch out designs. There's something about the damp, fuggy atmosphere that stimulates creative thought.

MARINE

Left There is something naturally uplifting about aquamarine and turquoise, the colors of sun-drenched seasides the world over.

Below Weathered aquamarine shutters and a stone sink make a simple and unpretentious rustic bathroom.

Seaside shades of aquamarine and turquoise—all those colors that lie between green and blue—strongly evoke a maritime setting. Bright, saturated versions of these colors appear in coastal areas wherever the light is strong—from traditional Greek Cycladic whitewashed houses, with their vivid greeny-blue woodwork, to Caribbean island villas, with their painted weatherboarding. It seems that whenever the sea is in view, there's a natural instinct to echo your surroundings in the colors you choose to live with.

How to use a marine palette

✸
These positive upbeat colors work well indoors, particularly in areas that have a good quality of natural light. Turquoise walls might be a little too full-on for living rooms, but they work well in more enclosed spaces where you don't spend so much time, such as bathrooms. Offset these strong shades with plenty of white.

✸
A subtler effect on the same theme can be achieved with faded shades of duck-egg blue, eau de nil, and greeny gray, which recreate the weatheredpalette typical of coastal areas in the northern hemisphere. These lighter shades make elegant backgrounds for living areas and are naturally space-enhancing.

✸
Anchor this color scheme with darker tones of gray or deep blue and accent with dashes of warm, sandy yellow or ocher.

COMPLEMENTARY SCHEMES

Left The electric pairing of red and green is exploited fully in this open-plan living area, with its vibrant red spatial divider and window wall partially glazed in green.

Below A subtler example of this reverberant pairing are these pendant lights, with their contrasting "stop" and "go" colored interiors.

Few color pairs are so hard-wired as opposites as green and red. From the universally used traffic signals—green for "go" and red for "stop"—to the ripe fruit or poisonous berry calling attention to itself from among lush, green foliage, this is a color combination with particular vibrancy. Like all complementary pairs, the purest and brightest versions of these colors are very reverberant when set against each other—almost painfully so.

Forest green and tomato red are a common combination in folk art, tartan, and traditional nordic interiors. For this reason, not to mention the association with Christmas, you need to exercise a degree of restraint when decorating with these colors, to avoid the risk of your home looking kitsch.

How to use green and red

❈
In muted form
Lighter or grayed shades of green and pale reds or rose are a more livable form of this pairing—plaster-pink walls and gray-green cabinets, for example.

❈
In small doses
Pairings of strong green and red are not for large-scale consumption. But their cheerful vibrancy sings out in soft furnishings and accessories, such as flat-weave rugs and runners, pillow covers, blankets, and throws. Striped, spotted, checked, or plaid designs give a contemporary look.

❈
In proportion
Restrict the element of red in the combination to small touches of accent color—as a binding or trim, or as decorative object.

Below A built-in storage wall with square niches and closed cupboards features an interplay of green and yellow. The blue rug is an anchoring element. The suspended acrylic chair is Eero Aarnio's Bubble design, which dates from 1968.

Right Blue and green, contrary to the old saying, make excellent decorative partners. Here they are mediated by warm wood tones.

CLASSIC
CONRAN
COLOR
CELADON

From childhood onwards, I've always had a love of craft, of making things by hand in wood, metal and clay. During World War II, when we lived in the country, my mother let me build a wood-fired kiln in the garden. I can well remember the thrill of opening it up after its first firing and discovering that almost all of the pots I had made were intact. This passion was further developed at Bryanston, where I went to school. There I was taught pottery, sculpture, and metalwork by a brilliantly inspiring man called Don Potter, who had himself been taught by Eric Gill and was influenced by Bernard Leach. It's not surprising that some of my most treasured possessions are pots, including a beautiful celadon bowl made for me by the Japanese ceramicist Kawase Shinobu.

Celadon, which lends its name to a type of ceramics and their characteristic pale grayish-green color, was originally developed in China, and the technique later spread to Japan, Korea, and other Asian countries. One component of the glaze is wood ash. What I particularly love about the color, aside from its delicacy, is what you might call its elusiveness. Like all shades that combine elements of other colors, its appearance changes with the quality of light. In the office of my new London apartment, one wall is lined with a series of shelves in deepening shades of gray—celadon bowls are arranged along the lowest one. Those pictured here are by South African master-potter Anthony Shapiro.

red

red

Red is both nature's lure and warning rolled into one—the ripe apple and the poisonous berry. The color of blood, danger, and high alert, red is associated with a whole range of strong emotions, from anger and alarm to passion and guilt. It's not for the faint-hearted.

If the color red has such powerful connotations, it's hardly surprising. Red is literally "in your face." A so-called "advancing" color, it corresponds to the longer wavelengths of light, which in turn demand the highest degree of adjustment from our eyes. We interpret this physical shock or jolt to the system as various forms of stimulus, from excitement to alarm. "Stop" signs all around the world are red for a good reason—so, too, are posters advertising sales.

Yet there are notable cultural differences in the way red is perceived. Even in this day and age, getting married in red might seem a step too far for most Westerners, but this is not the case in India, where it is the traditional color of wedding saris. In China, too, red is considered a very lucky color and is widely used in celebrations.

Choosing the right shade of any color is always important; all the more so in the case of red because it is so eye-catching. Scarlet veers a little way towards orange, vermilion even more so. Crimson has a hint of blue. Deep reds include burgundy and ruby, along with maroon, which is brownish. Softer reds, such as berry colors and warm, earthy tones, are more user-friendly.

RED
DYES
AND
PIGMENTS

Left An airy, white bedroom is given extra visual warmth by the red-and-white bedcover and the red leather sling seat.

Below The red-enameled sides of this freestanding bathtub pick up on the more subdued red checkerboard flooring.

Red is the oldest color. There is widespread evidence of the use of red pigments going back tens of thousands of years—in cave paintings, in tombs, as decoration on pottery, and as body art. By the 16th century, there were well over 50 different recipes for creating red pigments and dyes—the quest, as ever, was for an intense color that was non-fading.

✳
Red ocher or hematite comes from iron oxide, one of the most common minerals on earth. This earthy pigment was used to decorate the artefacts of many different civilizations and is a feature of numerous cave paintings.

✳
Cinnabar comes from the highly toxic mercury sulphide, a mineral found in volcanic areas and near hot springs; it produces a brilliant vermilion. Chinese lacquerware was traditionally decorated with cinnabar.

✳
Cochineal red, or carmine, comes from the blood of crushed female cochineal beetles. The earliest use of this pigment was in ancient Peru, but the Spanish controlled its supply for use in dress and decoration for many centuries.

✳
Kermes, a genus of scale insects common in Persia and Mesopotamia, was used to make crimson or scarlet.

✳
The root of the common madder plant was used to make a dullish red-brown.

ACCENTS AND FOCAL POINTS

Left I tend to think that most kitchen surfaces and finishes should be kept relatively restrained. It's a busy area and you want the focus to fall on food and displays of fresh fruit and vegetables. This red Arne Jacobsen chair provides just the right touch of accent color.

Below This cabinet, decorated in evocative Chinese red, lends an interior a subtle Eastern flavour. Red is considered a celebratory color throughout much of Asia, and traditional Chinese lacquerwork was decorated with cinnabar, which gave a brilliant shade of vermilion.

Red is the supreme accent color. Just as a dab of red lipstick draws disproportionately more attention than the surface area it covers, the smallest touch of red in the interior will sing out of its background. These days many people would fight shy of decorating an entire room in red or using a strong, bright red as a background. Experimenting with red accents and focal points is a great way to enjoy the vitality of the color without the risk of overstimulation.

✣ Glossy finishes increase the impact of any color. Red enameled pots and pans, kitchen ranges, and red refrigerators, and kettles make eye-catching accents and focal points in the kitchen, as do red glass backsplashes and cabinet fronts.

✣ Red dining chairs are very convivial—we sold many red Magistretti rush-bottomed chairs at Habitat in the early days. Simple junk-shop finds, such as plain wooden tables and chairs, can be brightened up with a coat of paint. Lacquered chests of drawers have an Eastern quality.

✣ Upholstery is a good way of using red on a slightly larger scale. Red used to upholster Jacobsen's Egg Chair (1958), for example, emphasizes its cocooning organic form. Bench seating, banquettes, club chairs, and sofas covered in red leather combine a dash of accent color along with a pleasing smell and tactile quality.

✣ Quilts, pillow covers, and throws bring visual warmth to bedrooms and seating areas.

✣ Red runners and flat-weave stair carpets create vibrant pathways up the stairs and along corridors.

✣ Translucent red shades for pendant and table lamps give a rosy glow to lighting, as well as being accents in themselves.

Below As a siren shade, red always attracts a great deal of attention, even in small doses. The base of this cabinet with its top-mounted sink adds great flair to an essentially monochromatic bathroom.

Right The merest sliver of red—as displayed by the padded linings of these seat shells—has a hospitable, celebratory quality.

GRAPHIC SCHEMES

Left Sleek and confident, this bold contemporary kitchen scheme features a glossy scarlet island unit as its focal point. A similarly reflective finish is used on the brickwork behind the worktop.

Below Here a plane of red is used as a spatial marker defining a shower area. The introduction of the bright yellow chair adds punch to the strong combination of red, white, and black.

One way of handling the energy of red is to surround it with plenty of breathing space, in the form of white walls and pale or natural flooring. Red may be no less eye-catching in areas where the rest of the decoration is restrained or neutral, but it won't overpower you. A further advantage is that by restricting red to relatively small touches, you can afford to ring the changes when you tire of it.

How to use red in graphic schemes

✳
In textiles, white domesticates every color with which it is paired. This is particularly true of red, which loses some of its heat in simple checked, striped, and spotted designs—the homespun appeal of checked gingham being a case in point. Red-and-white patterns are innately hospitable and cheerful. "Poppy,", a stylized textile design produced by Marimekko, is a contemporary floral fabric with immense appeal.

✳
The addition of black or gray makes for a more interesting, sharper palette, with an added degree of formality. At its starkest, this combination has overtones of Constructivism. Mix in yellow or blue, and the combination evokes midcentury decoration.

✳
The juxtaposition of strong primaries with neutrals is given added punch when color is used in planes or when patterns are geometric. A red feature wall signaling an eating area within an open-plan layout, red tiling lining a shower, and a red rug anchoring a seating arrangement all use the color for spatial definition.

CLASSIC REDS

Below Built-in storage faced in red echoes the warm, reddish tones of the hardwood flooring.

Right Oxblood is a traditional, deep red that is easy to live with in large doses, even as a background color. Where brighter reds might be too assertive and attention-seeking, these duller shades produce a warm and intimate atmosphere.

For our ancestors, red was such an expensive color that it quickly became a signifier of status and prestige. From the Renaissance onwards, the walls of palace staterooms were typically hung with red silk damask—offset, naturally, with plenty of gold—in a lavish display of power and influence intended to impress onlookers and heighten their excitement. Dining rooms, picture galleries, and other reception rooms in grand houses continued to feature red decoration well into the 19th century. I must say that when I visited some of these stately homes as a schoolboy, I was thoroughly repelled by them, much preferring the no-nonsense simplicity of the servants' quarters below stairs.

EASY-GOING COMBINATIONS

Red rooms may not carry such connotations of wealth and exclusivity today, but they are undoubtedly highly charged. A more livable version of this type of decoration—and one that is less about impressing the neighbors than creating a sense of warmth and intimacy—is to opt for richer, darker shades, everything from berry reds and spicy reds to burgundy and oxblood. Even in large doses, these colors are hospitable rather than assertive—more likely to put you in a cozy frame of mind than to set your pulses racing.

Decorative schemes that rely heavily on red tend to work best in rooms that are used predominantly in the evening and that are relatively small and self-contained; this is not an approach you'll want to adopt in an open-plan layout. Red is especially appealing when lit by candlelight and firelight and makes a wonderfully snug background for entertaining or relaxing.

❖ Oxblood, or *sang de boeuf*, is a deep, traditional red, which makes a rich, enveloping background, particularly in country settings or in paneled rooms. Sage-green and ultramarine make good partners.

❖ Paisley-patterned fabric, flat-weave kelims, and many other types of Eastern textiles display rich combinations of warm, spicy colors, from cinnamon to paprika. You can use a large rug as a focal point for a seating arrangement, or layer different textiles for a richer effect. Complement such a mix with blue-green.

❖ Maroon, cranberry, and cherry red are sophisticated shades that work well with contemporary décor. In particular, they lend warmth to interiors that feature hard-edged or industrial materials, such as concrete, stainless steel ,and exposed brick.

❖ Vibrant complementary schemes feature red with green. At its most electric, this pairing needs plenty of breathing space—a gentler version relies on slightly faded or dulled shades to suggest a summer's garden.

Left A wall painted in a rich shade of burgundy lends coziness to a bathroom. The white bathtub resting on shaped wooden blocks and the white mosaic flooring provide neutral breathing space.

Below An expanse of lacquered red wall, mirror, white tiling ,and black marble sink and countertop make a well-balanced combination. The Cross Cabinet (1992) is by Swedish designer Thomas Eriksson for the Italian manufacturer Cappellini.

PINK

Left Pretty in pink: a pale, elegant version of the shade combines well with the dusty-blue walls and ceiling of this kitchen with its vibrant yellow cabinets.

Below Pink does not have to be relegated to the boudoir. A wall of seamless built-in cabinets, painted spun sugar pink, provides a surprising take on kitchen décor.

Pink is much more than a watered-down version of red. From the rosy tints of a dawn sky to the exuberance of cherry blossom, it can be soft and flattering, soothing and delicate or decidedly shocking, depending on the shade. Some pinks can be a little sickly-looking. Peach, a staid favorite of the old-fashioned furnishings department, is often insipid, especially in large doses. But earthier plaster pinks have all the robust character of a fresco.

In the West, pink has long been heavily marketed as a feminine color, a boudoir association that can be a little difficult to overcome in the interior. Funnily enough, in the 19th century pink was thought to be a suitable color for boys, because it was a lighter shade of red, which was seen as assertive and active.

How to use pink

✿ As a focal point
A jolt of shocking pink makes an electric focal point—in a self-contained space such as a bathroom, for example, or as the color of cladding on a kitchen-island unit.

✿ As a background
Dusty shades of pink make warm, flattering backgrounds in areas where the quality of light is less than ideal. Pink-washed walls have a rustic quality.

✿ With clashing colors
Pink, red, and orange make vivid clashing schemes, as exemplified in the geometric-patterned carpets and wallpaper designed by David Hicks in the 1960s.

✿ With cool colors
In combination with other cool or bluish shades, such as turquoise, silvery gray, and lime green, pink is elegant and sophisticated.

✿ Magenta
Magenta or fuchsia, a strong, hot, pinkish purple, is a wild, untamable shade and a little goes a long way. Magenta made its first appearance as an aniline dye in the mid-19th century and is named after a battle during the Crimean War.

SUGARED ALMONDS

Left A collection of midcentury modern ceramics displays the sugared-almond palette typical of the period.

Below When these sweet colors are used in geometric patterns, rather than representational or floral designs, the effect is fresh and pretty without being overly twee.

The delicate freshness of rose pink, leaf green, and white is a color combination with a long decorative history. One of the most classic examples is English chintz, which was itself a borrowing from Mughal textiles of all descriptions, from carpets to wall hangings. Translated into (often glazed) cotton printed with designs typically featuring flowers and foliage, chintz came to epitomize the genteel British drawing room. Swathes of the fabric were manufactured and used as upholstery, typically in the form of loose covers. Wallpapers were also produced in the same colors and designs.

The risk with any scheme based on these soft, sweet colors is that it can be a little too pretty-pretty, all the more so if you include designs that are essentially figurative, such as small, sprigged repeats. One solution is to opt for patterns that are bold and overscaled; another is to choose stylized contemporary versions.

✣ Sugared-almond colors are often a feature of mid-century modern ceramics, such as those produced by the British manufacturer Poole Pottery. A collection of stoneware plates, dishes, jugs, and bowls is a good way of indulging your taste for such shades while retaining a contemporary edge.

✣ Stripes, checks, and other geometric designs display the essential elegance of the combination without running the risk of tweeness.

CLASSIC
CONRAN
COLOR
CHINESE RED

Symbolic of eternity and the life force, red has been an important color in Chinese culture since ancient times, specifically vermilion made from powdered cinnabar. This pigment and its later synthetic equivalent was used to color lacquerware, which began to be exported to the West in the 17th and 18th centuries in ever greater quantities, giving rise to the term "Chinese red." The richness of the shade was enhanced by the glossy varnish, which was derived from a resin. Both pigment and resin were highly toxic, as were many early sources of intense color.

Red is always eye-catching—and hospitable. To my mind, a red dining chair invites you to sit down, gather round the table and celebrate. It gives a meal a sense of occasion.

The Grand Prix chair, designed in 1957 by Arne Jacobsen, was originally known as the Model 3130—the name change came after the design won the prestigious Grand Prix at the Triennale di Milano. It is available in a range of finishes, from oak and walnut veneer to colored ash. In Chinese red, this design classic becomes a vibrant spatial marker, the color adding extra punch to its graphic lines.

Like many of Jacobsen's dining chairs, the seat, or shell, is made of layers of thin wood veneer pressure-moulded into shape. The original design featured chrome legs: this version with wooden legs was recently reintroduced by Fritz Hansen, the Danish furniture company that now manufactures Jacobsen's designs.

yellow

yellow

Yellow is a positive, sunny color that is guaranteed to lift the spirits. Depending on the precise shade, it can be elegant and refined, rich and lavish, or vibrant and eye-catching—both to us and to other creatures. Yellow is the most common flower color because it attracts pollinators.

Like red, yellow is an ancient color, with the earliest ocher pigments being derived from clay deposits. Saffron and turmeric are other natural sources of yellow that have been used over the centuries. Saffron comes from the red stigma of crocuses. Because so many flowers are required to produce the tiniest amount of saffron, the dye (along with the food color and flavouring) is very expensive. Turmeric, as anyone who has ever cooked a curry knows, stains readily. Unlike saffron, it is cheap and widely available.

Chrome yellow, the natural form of lead chromate, is a pigment that was discovered in the early 19th century. The bright, strong shade rapidly became the rage among the well-to-do. One of the most famous examples of the yellow rooms that were so fashionable during this period is the sun-drenched drawing room at Sir John Soane's Museum in Lincoln's Inn Fields, London where chrome-yellow walls are boldly set off with narrow bands of black and accents of red.

SUNSHINE YELLOW

Left The bright yellow painted interior of this glass-fronted cabinet is the perfect foil for a graphic display featuring Fornasetti plates and silver platters.

Below Metallic finishes, such as stainless steel, go very well with bright yellow. Here a Corian countertop has an inset steel sink.

Bright and bold, sunny or lemon yellows lighten interiors and spread warmth and good feeling around. Because these yellows are not quite as insistent as reds and oranges, you can afford to be a little more generous with their application without running the risk of tiring the eyes.

How to use sunshine yellow

✳ As splashes of accent color in decorative displays, pictures, and colored glassware. A bowl of lemons on a sunny kitchen counter is no less effective for being simple and impromptu.

✳ In self-contained spaces, such as wet rooms and bathrooms, or for entryways and landings.

✳ Yellow gains extra intensity when the finish is glossy and reflective, as in laminated finishes, or where it is used in translucent backlit panels.

✳ As a spatial definition within an open-plan layout—to pick out a study area, for example.

✳ These pure forms of bright yellow work particularly well in combination with strong blues; when you think of the sun shining in a clear blue sky, it's easy to appreciate why.

LONG-DISTANCE VISION

Taxis, school buses, hi-vis jackets, and construction equipment are often colored yellow so that they can be readily identified at a distance. All complementary pairs of colors vibrate when they are set against each other. Yellow's complementary color is violet, the color of the horizon, which means that a yellow object that is far away will be easier to spot than one of a different shade.

Below Strong, eye-catching color works well as a spatial divider, announcing the presence of a different zone within an open-plan layout. To be effective, sunshine-yellow needs plenty of ... sunshine.

Right Industrial-style metal pendant lights in bold, uplifting yellow add a dash of primary color to a monochromatic kitchen with stainless-steel fittings and fixtures.

MELLOW YELLOW

Left Our bedroom in our house in the country has rich yellow walls, a bespoke finish created using layers of dappled glazing; they are a very optimistic sight to behold first thing in the morning.

Below left Paler shades of yellow, such as the bleached-out straw-colored tones, are very elegant, especially in combination with gray and white.

Below right Primrose yellow has an airy, reflective quality, which makes it ideal for enhancing the sense of space in compact areas, such as this galley kitchen.

When you are using yellow in larger, more immersive doses, particularly as a background, you may find that you need to experiment a little more than usual. Because yellow is so strongly associated with sunshine, it's even more important to ensure that you pick the right shade to go with the prevailing conditions of natural light: you are more likely to notice if you get it wrong. Yellow can be sickly—in fact, somewhat jaundiced—in rooms where the light levels are low or have a bluish cast. The yellow walls of our south-facing bedroom in our house in the country did not come straight out of the tin, but were the result of layers of stippled glazes built up to achieve the desired result.

Yellow's innate cheerfulness makes it a natural choice for rooms where people gather. In a family kitchen, it is uplifting without being overly demanding. In a dining area, it evokes a hospitable feeling—think of Claude Monet's famous yellow dining room in his house in Giverny, where the walls make a vivid backdrop to the artist's collection of Japanese woodblock prints.

Pale and interesting shades of yellow can be easier to handle than the rich, buttery tones. Primrose or straw-colored backgrounds have a quiet elegance and work very well with a range of other shades, particularly grays, whites, and off-greens.

EARTH
TONES

Left Two shades of ocher, red and yellow, bring a rustic quality to this hallway with its beamed, planked ceiling.

Right A harmonious, earthy scheme features shades of light and midbrown, along with mustard-yellow upholstery on the teak-framed sofa. This is a typical midcentury modern palette.

Ocher and raw sienna are earthy yellows that are soft, easy on the eye and adaptable to a wide range of applications. Because these shades were easy to produce from pigments derived from clay and sand, they have cropped up in exterior and interior decoration around the world for centuries. As backgrounds, earthy yellows are warm and glowing, making the most of natural light. Mustard-yellow is a slightly more sophisticated version. None of these colors are the least bit eggy.

In contemporary interiors, ocher, brick red, and black comprise a robust palette with midcentury modern overtones. Some years ago, I was fortunate enough to stay at Villa Sarabhai, a house in Ahmedabad, India, designed by Le Corbusier in the 1950s. The interior reveals a masterful interplay of surface and texture, along with a strong, earthy palette expressed both in paint and exposed materials: brick, black stone, red ocher, white, yellow, and green. Incidentally, Le Corbusier did not subscribe to the standard formula of using warm colors where light was low, and cool colors in sunnier spaces. Instead, he deliberately set out to enhance architectural volume by bringing bright areas further forward with reds and yellows, and pushing dark areas further back with blues.

GRAPHIC SCHEMES

Left Bright yellow contributes a playful, graphic quality to this reclaimed vintage cabinet. The little architectural-style towers to the right are made of Eames's House of Cards, decks of cards featuring found images, patterns, and colors, which were first issued in 1952.

Below Schemes that feature strong primary yellow and black have great sophistication. Here a glossy yellow floor and countertop are contrasted with a sleek black bathtub surround, backsplash, and cupboard doors.

In its purest, clearest form, yellow is a primary—a color that cannot be made by mixing other colors together. This makes it a bold, graphic choice for adding impact in contemporary interiors.

How to combine yellow

✽

The combination of yellow and white is fresh as a daisy. Yellow-and-white curtains with the sun shining through them look cheerful and breezy.

✽

Yellow and black, on the other hand, has more sophisticated, Eastern overtones. This pairing was common in Modernist interiors, with some of the yellow being supplied in the form of yellowish wood paneling and flooring. Yellow, white, black, and gray makes a very subtle and elegant palette, with the primary color giving the neutral shades focus and vivacity.

✽

Schemes composed entirely of primary colors have a bold simplicity. These building blocks of color strike a lively, cheerful note in children's rooms—elsewhere you may need to exercise more restraint. When organized into geometric panels of various sizes bordered by black, the effect is reminiscent of the Eames House (1945–9), where color articulates the kit-of-parts approach to construction. A simpler way of using the combination is to restrict the primaries to accents and details, such as rugs, pillow covers, or decorative displays.

Below Custom-built, separate "hers" and "hers" storage and study areas are defined by their bright yellow and green interiors.

Right Primary colors are positive and cheerful in children's bedrooms. The painted finish of the bunk bed, striped rug, and world map are elements that are easy to change when children grow older and want their own say in decorative matters.

CLASSIC
CONRAN
COLOR
CHROME YELLOW

What could be more cheerful than the sunflower? Originally a native of the Americas, *Helianthus annuus* was introduced to Europe in the 17th century and has since become a common sight in summer gardens. The graphic, almost childlike simplicity of the large flower head and its bright, positive color strike a note of pure optimism. But the sunflower is not simply decorative. It is widely cultivated for its oil and seeds, and is also a component of silage and animal feed. Beautiful and useful—that's a combination that appeals to me.

The *Sunflowers* series, produced by Vincent van Gogh in the late 1880s, when he was living in the south of France, are among the most famous flower paintings in the world.

They are drenched in the heat and light of le Midi. From the letters the artist wrote to his brother, who kept him supplied with tubes of pigment from a Parisian manufacturer, we know that he used chrome yellow to paint the flower heads. Chrome yellow was a relatively new pigment at the time, first produced at the beginning of the 19th century, when its vibrancy and opacity made it all the rage in fashionable interiors. To make his sunflowers shine even brighter, van Gogh mixed chrome yellow with white pigments. What he could not have foreseen was that in so doing he initiated a chemical reaction that would eventually turn his sunflowers dull and brown—one of the many ironies in the history of color.

naturals

naturals

The natural palette, which runs the gamut from the pale shades of biscuit and cream through to the dark tones of mahogany and burnt umber, puts the emphasis squarely on material character. It's not that these shades can't be expressed in paint finishes, stains, and furnishing fabrics, but that they are more usefully and effectively introduced in the form of surfaces and finishes, where they will register primarily as texture, bringing depth of character to the interior.

Brown and all its associated tones are not part of the visible spectrum. These are colors that come from mixtures of other, purer shades, with or without the addition of white and black. For centuries, up until the arrival of cheap synthetic colors, this muted, often muddy palette was common in ordinary households as a matter of necessity. Today, however, it speaks more of sophistication and a certain degree of luxury, whether in a town or country setting. Natural materials—marble, granite, limestone, and hardwood—are far from the cheapest options, although they do repay the initial investment and the maintenance required for their upkeep with years of serviceable use. But perhaps the most persuasive argument in their favor is that time and wear do not degrade them, adding instead a patina of use that is very appealing.

STONE

Left "Honesty of construction" was a guiding principle of William Morris and the Arts and Crafts movement during the 19th century. These walls of exposed original stonework have their own integrity.

Below Slate tiles with a ridged, riven finish have been used to line this shower. Unlike other forms of stone, slate is naturally stain- and water-resistant.

In the form of flooring, cladding, countertops. and work surfaces, stone brings a sense of permanence and integrity to the interior. Although some types of stone come in surprisingly strong colors, including green, pink. and tomato red, what most people value are the cool, natural shades of biscuit, sand, and gray-brown, tones that are naturally light- and space-enhancing.

TYPES OF STONE

❊ **Granite** Typically mottled and flecked, granite is the hardest, densest and toughest material in domestic use.

❊ **Marble** Once synonymous with the height of luxury, marble can simply suggest mindless ostentation if not handled with a degree of restraint. Pure marble is white; the presence of other minerals, such as iron oxides, results in a range of other colors, some of which are quite striking. The feature that is most characteristic, however, is marble's cloudy translucency, cracks, and veining.

❊ **Limestone** Most types of limestone are cool and pale in color, ranging from off-white to light gold, while surfaces are often flecked or show fossilized traces of animal or vegetable life.

❊ **Travertine** A very strong type of stone, often used in construction, travertine has a pitted surface and comes in a range of cool whites, off-whites, grays, and browns. My bathroom at Barton Court has a beautiful gray-brown travertine floor.

❊ **Sandstone** As its name suggests, sandstone comes in a range of sandy browns and grayish browns. Yorkstone is one of the best-known types and is much in demand for outdoor paving.

❊ **Slate** Waterproof and wear-resistant, slate is available in dark, moody colors such as indigo and purplish gray. Depending on how it is finished, the surface texture can be smooth and polished or ridged and riven.

Sealing
❊
Most types of stone are porous to some degree; some are highly so. Therefore, sealing is generally required to prevent staining.

USES OF STONE

Most types of stone come in a range of formats—slabs and tiles of varying thickness to suit particular applications. An important consideration to bear in mind is weight. These materials are dense and heavy, and subfloors or cabinet construction may need to be strengthened to bear the load. Professional installation will almost always be required.

✲ **Flooring** Both outdoors and in, stone makes a classic, beautiful floor with great staying power. Honed or riven finishes, which provide a bit of grip, are better underfoot than those that are highly polished. Irregular slabs and tiles have a rustic appeal, while large regular formats are cool and contemporary.

✲ **Fittings and detail** One of the most traditional uses of stone in the home is in the form of fire surrounds and mantelpieces made of marble. Slate shelving in kitchens and pantries has also long been a way of providing natural refrigeration. Today, stone sinks and bathtubs have a timeless quality.

✲ **Counters** Granite, because it is so hard-wearing, makes excellent kitchen work surfaces. For seamless results, counters should have integral splashbacks. Because they are cool to the touch, marble slabs inset into counters make good surfaces for rolling pastry.

✲ **Cladding** Thinner stone tiles, specifically designed for walls, make elegant and practical backdrops in bathrooms, wet rooms, and shower enclosures.

WOOD

Left Oriented strand board (OSB) is wood at its most raw and unfinished. These economical manufactured panels, often used to board up store fronts, have a back-to-basics quality.

Below At the other end of the spectrum, hardwood veneer makes an elegant and sophisticated finish.

Wood is a versatile and varied material. Hardwoods, such as oak, beech, maple, and walnut, and softwoods, such as pine, have been used to construct, decorate, and furnish houses around the world since the first settlements. Today, with many hardwood species on the endangered list and deforestation a major environmental issue, it is important to buy timber from sustainable sources whenever possible.

❖ **Hardwoods** The most attractive, durable, and expensive types of wood are hardwoods. Color, grain, and patterning vary widely, from pale ash with its straight grain to dark, figured walnut. Many hardwoods are used as veneers over cheaper softwood panels or carcasses.

❖ **Softwoods** Fir, pine, and spruce are all examples of softwoods that are widely used in construction. Typically pale, close-grained, and knotty, they are generally not as hard-wearing as hardwoods and must be treated to improve their resistance to moisture and pests.

❖ **Manufactured woods** These products contain wood in varying proportions, often in the form of timber waste, formed into panels or boards using heat, glue, resins, and pressure. Unlike blockboard and fiberboard, which tend to be used behind the scenes in construction, plywood is increasingly valued for its cool, contemporary aesthetic. Two common types of plywood are birch-faced or all-birch.

USES OF WOOD

When it comes to construction, decoration, and furnishing, it's almost easier to list what wood hasn't been used for than to give an account of all its applications. However, where wood makes a positive statement, it is generally used on a fairly large scale and in such a way as to bring out its texture and grain.

I have a particular affection for the material. Benchmark, our woodworking company based at my house in the country, is a supplier of many wooden products, from furniture to bespoke fittings. It has just completed a fascinating project in conjunction with the American Hardwood Export Council, which paired the designs of well-known architects and designers with the expertise of young craftspeople.

Below Wood lends itself to a variety of finishes, from painting and sealing to bleaching and staining. In this bedroom, the lightened tones of the matchboard paneling and stripped floorboards retain the natural warmth of the material without being overly dominant.

Right Warm wood wall paneling, a whitewashed ceiling, and casement windows inset with colored glass give the country cottage aesthetic a fresh, modern update.

✣ **Flooring** Wooden floors are available in a range of formats, systems, materials, and prices—from solid hardwood made of oak or similar species to wood laminates with barely any wood content. As is the case with many natural materials, color is not the principal story. Instead, it's rhythm and texture—from narrow planking to wide boards, from herringbone wood block to basketweave.

✣ **Paneling and cladding** Wood paneling generates a great sense of warmth and intimacy. Traditionally, rectangular panels are framed by rails and stiles. Matchboarding and tongue-and-groove have a more rustic quality.

✣ **Fixtures and fitting** Wood is used all around the home in many and varied applications. At both French doors and windows, solid wooden shutters are treasured period features in Colonial houses. In warm climates, wooden slatted louvers filter strong sunlight while allowing the air to circulate. Built-in storage cabinets in kitchens and bathrooms invariably make widespread use of wood, both solid and veneered, while thick work surfaces and bathroom sink tops are often made from the heartwood of certain hardwood species, such as beech and oak. In addition, open stairways often feature thick, cantilevered wooden treads.

MINIMAL

Left Less is definitely more when you have a great architectural space to play with and good conditions of natural light. Touches of washed-out pinks, grays, and browns add a human touch, without detracting from the pared-back approach.

Below Successful minimal interiors display a high level of detailing, as well as surfaces and finishes that more than merit the exposure, such as this pristine ceramic tiled floor.

Minimal interiors take inspiration from a number of sources; arguably the most important is the traditional Japanese house. Sliding paper shoji screens, tatami mats, and the occasional low stool or table create serene, contemplative spaces, in which you become acutely conscious of the quality of sound and the play of light.

I'm not the world's greatest minimalist—I prefer to surround myself with more to look at. But I do appreciate that in the hands of great designers such as John Pawson, pared-down interiors have a beauty all their own. In many cases, these interiors are heavily reliant on the best natural materials for their effect; the surfaces and finishes that remain on view must be worthy of attention. An empty room carpeted in beige is dreary, but the same space with a pale limestone floor has a different character entirely. Similarly, the level of detailing has to be of a very high order. The junctions between different surfaces or planes and the fashioning of built-in elements, such as walls of seamless cupboards, must be exact for the simple reason that there is little else to distract your attention from them.

MODERN ORGANIC

Left Entirely lined in wood, a wet room open to the elements is bathed in natural light. Wood that is exposed to water must be treated to prevent rot. Teak is naturally water-resistant, but you must ensure that it comes from approved suppliers.

Below Dark reclaimed floorboards used to panel the wall behind the bed make a warm backdrop. Sourcing materials from sustainable or second-hand sources is all part of the ethos of modern organic.

The natural palette comes into its own in decorative schemes that might loosely be termed "modern organic." Here the strong, clean lines and open-plan layouts of contemporary design are partnered with materials that wear their natural credentials with pride and contribute warmth and character to the interior. Bright color is not banished entirely, but it definitely takes a back seat in favor of textural variety. The not-so-hidden agenda is often a concern to source materials that are from fair-trade and sustainable sources, along with one-off products and designs that have been handcrafted.

Modern organic elements

✳ Textiles and soft furnishings with an overt weave or homespun quality, such as raw or unbleached linen in shades of taupe and ecru, sheepskin throws and rugs, felted blankets and pillow covers, and knitted throws.

✳ Extensive use of wood as flooring and cladding, either in the form of new or reclaimed floorboards and paneled walls. Bleached or lightened wood keeps the effect airy and spacious.

✳ Natural-fiber floor coverings, such as sisal, seagrass, and coir, make an alternative to wool or wool-mix carpeting.

✳ A deliberate avoidance of synthetic materials, surfaces, and finishes.

✳ Simple, rough-hewn furniture, such as plain, scrubbed wooden tables and benches.

✳ Plenty of indoor greenery, in the form of flourishing house plants, grouped for impact.

LIGHT INDUSTRIAL

Left This converted loft features key elements of the light industrial aesthetic—a restrained natural palette, original brick walls with a light whitewashing to reveal the underlying texture, and an absence of fussy decoration and furnishing.

Below The professional kitchen, with its reliance on sleek stainless-steel fittings and fixtures, is another version of the look. The wall-mounted light is the Tolomeo, designed by Michele de Lucchi and Giancarlo Fassina in 1986 for Artemide.

Ever since the first commercial and industrial buildings were colonized in city centres in the 1970s, the loft aesthetic has refused to go away. Today it is more prevalent than ever in fashionable cafés, shops, and restaurants, as much as in homes. It is perhaps a stretch to call such schemes "natural," in that many of the materials exposed to view are often highly processed—concrete, for example, or steel—even if they are reused and reclaimed. But they do remain natural in terms of being largely unadorned—the "honesty of construction" of the Arts and Crafts movement lives on in the dynamic modern urban warehouse.

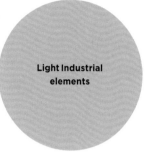

Light Industrial elements

✳ Walls and floors stripped back to their original state to bring texture to the fore—exposed brickwork, for instance. Similarly, ducting, steel joists, beams, and pipework are often left on view.

✳ Rugged industrial materials are pressed into service to make fitted and unfitted elements—the cast-concrete kitchen counter, for example, or the steel spiral staircase.

✳ Furnishings and fittings include products that started life in industrial, commercial, or retail contexts, such as metal pendant light shades, steel lockers and filing cabinets, refectory tables, and such like.

✳ As with Hi Tech, the previous incarnation of this industrial aesthetic, strong primary colors are used as vivid accents against the essentially muted background.

This page Industrial-style pendant lights and robust metal-faced custom-made cabinets create a workable, no-nonsense kitchen.

CLASSIC
CONRAN
COLOR
ECRU

Pale natural tones—the colors of sand, stone, and bleached wood—are very useful for introducing understated elegance into the interior, especially when these colors are expressed in a material form, rather than as a painted finish. As always, you need to take into account existing light conditions. In underlit areas of the home, some of these shades can be a little drab; in brighter rooms, they make good backgrounds or mediators between stronger, more vibrant tones.

Beige is a catch-all term for many of these off-whites and near-whites. Over the years, it has acquired connotations of conformity and blandness—a safe non-choice for those who fight shy of the dynamism of color altogether. Much more interesting is the crisper, cooler shade called ecru, a natural tone that has more depth and presence. Interestingly, both beige and ecru are French terms for undyed fabric or material, beige referring to natural wool and ecru to unbleached linen or silk. Taupe, another French term, is an even darker shade, the color of moleskin.

For centuries, linen used to be bleached in the open air by exposing the fabric to sunshine. Nowadays it is chemically treated in a process that has a significant impact on the environment—so the choice of unbleached linen is natural in more ways than one. I very much like the raw quality of unbleached linen, as well as its tendency to crease and wrinkle. Along with stoneware pottery, it goes very well with the simple, rustic aesthetic of the country kitchen.

neutrals

neutrals

In its purest form, white might be said to contain all colors. Black, on the other hand, represents color's total absence. In between the two are innumerable shades of gray—certainly more than 50. Together, they comprise the neutral palette.

Neutral tones and shades are indispensable in decorative schemes—they literally provide essential light and shade. White for breathing space, black for definition, and gray for tonality: each works as a foil for stronger, more vivid colors. In fact, the only way you can use some exceptionally punchy shades without the risk of overkill is by offsetting them against a neutral background.

Neutral colors—or "non-colors"—do not always have to play a supporting role. In the right context and with the right application, they can make powerful statements in their own right. White-on-white schemes, mysterious black backgrounds, and silvery, shimmery combinations of grays can all be much more intriguing than the word "neutral" would at first suggest.

It is easy enough to appreciate how difficult it was for our ancestors to produce bright, stable colors from animal, vegetable, and mineral sources. What is perhaps more surprising is that for many centuries certain neutral tones, particularly pure black, were equally hard to come by. Those neutrals that were more commonly and readily found—as is the case with lead white—often brought with them a toxic legacy.

WHITE

Left Pure-white schemes take a little extra care to assemble, as white can look very different according to texture and material. Here the white décor comes chiefly in the form of paintwork and upholstery—the natural tones of wood prevent the effect from being too insipid.

Below left White has a traditional association with the kitchen, where it suggests good housekeeping and cleanliness. In this all-white kitchen even the wall-mounted lights have white enameled shades.

Below right In a highly built-in space, which many bathrooms are, white décor gives visual coherence.

Pure white, which approximates to light, theoretically contains all colors. White surfaces reflect almost all the wavelengths of light away from them. In the West, white has long been a symbol of purity—the white wedding originated as a statement about the chastity of the bride. In Eastern cultures, however, white has a strong association with death and illness. Many Asian countries mourn in white.

Today, white or off-white is one of the most common choices for backgrounds in the interior, but this wasn't always the case. In the days when color was expensive and difficult to achieve, white was regarded as both utilitarian and humdrum. When William Morris sang the praises of "honest whitewash" in the 19th century, he was effectively recommending to middle-class taste a workaday finish that was typically applied to below-stairs areas, as well as cowsheds and privies.

But white only really began to take off in fashionable circles with the arrival of electricity. Electric light was clean—unlike candlelight or gaslight, it did not discolor the walls. This meant that a white wall would remain that way for longer. In addition, electric light was revealing—dust and dirt could not be so easily disguised. The all-white interiors popularized by society decorators in the 1930s—achieved with the new pigment titanium white—were, in a sense, advertising the fact that their owners possessed sufficient means to keep them that way.

BREATHING SPACE

Below White is the supreme mediator, providing a clean contrast or breathing space when set against any color. These white built-in bathroom units are self-effacing.

Right White painted floorboards, with their slightly distressed finish, make an effective foil for mid-gray walls and rustic furniture.

White walls and woodwork are widespread in contemporary décor and it's not hard to see why. White enhances the sense of space and makes the most of whatever natural light is available—and space and light are the two aspects we prize the most in our interiors. It's also fair to say that white is commonly chosen as a fail-safe option. When we have hundreds of colors, tones, and shades available to us, the choice can be overwhelming and fear of making a mistake can hold us back.

Over the years, many of the interiors in my own houses have had white walls. I'm not saying that the same approach should be adopted as a rule of thumb—it just reflects my preferences. What I would suggest is that white walls make a good starting point for any decorative scheme. Living with the blank canvas of a plain background allows you to assess the quality of natural light at different times of the day and work out how to make the most of the assets that a particular room or space possesses. Then you can go on to make color choices armed with this knowledge.

White as a mediator

✻ At the risk of sounding dictatorial, white is the only color for bathroom fixtures.

✻ Base boards, doors, and other forms of interior trim, molding, or woodwork often look best painted white. This provides a crisp, fresh contrast with colored walls of any shade.

✻ Almost any color can be set against another if white is placed between them. White is the essential breathing space in many patterns, designs, and decorative schemes.

WHITER SHADES OF PALE

Left When the quality of natural light is this good—as well as the view – pristine white décor enhances the sense of wellbeing.

Below White décor accentuates the play of light and shade. Even small colored details, such as the green tubular metal chair frames, spring into life.

Any discussion about white naturally leads straight to the question: which white? Ivory, bone, vanilla, eggshell, milk, alabaster, pearl, snow—most whites are not pure, but contain the faintest traces of other colors, both warm and cool. The two most popular white paints are a case in point; magnolia is a warm off-white, while "brilliant" white has chillier tints of blue.

While many people tend to regard white as the easy option, the irony is that it is not always straightforward to choose the right white for a given location. Again, quality of light is the key factor. Cool whites suit sunny rooms, but you will need a warm tone of white where light levels are lower. Some years ago, when we redecorated Barton Court, our house in the country, we used five different shades of white, including a soft, chalky white in the living room and a chillier white in one of the bathrooms.

You may think such subtle distinctions are hardly worth worrying about. But human beings are exceptionally light-sensitive creatures, with sight being our dominant sense. These minute changes of tone, which translate as thousands of different shades of white, are perfectly distinguishable.

If the appearance of white varies according to light levels, this is even more the case when you factor different surfaces and materials into the equation. All-white schemes are soothing and almost otherworldly, yet they are among the most difficult to achieve. White tiles, white linen, white enameled finishes, and white painted floorboards will all show slight variations in tone. While it would be impossible to match each white with precision, it's as well to be aware that some off-whites will look grubby next to purer tones.

BLACK

Left A feature wall decorated in black wallpaper printed with an elusive, slightly iridescent floral design has great theatrical presence.

Below The rhythmic grid of white grouting gives this black tiled bathroom an inherent liveliness that it would otherwise lack if the surfaces were uniform and matt.

The ultimate non-color, black represents the complete absence of light and color. Unsurprisingly, its principal cultural associations are somber and funereal. Black is gloomy and Gothic.

In decoration, however, black can be an extremely useful means of adding definition to color schemes and providing graphic contrast. It sharpens up detail and introduces a note of formality.

The great English architect Sir Edwin Lutyens went further and often used black as the background color (or non-color) for reception rooms, set off with crisp white woodwork and crown moldings. This treatment caused as much of a stir then as it would today, but the results were far from depressing. The black, which was painted over layers of different colored undercoats, had great depth and character, and its glossy finish had a lively, reflective quality.

BLACK DYE

While natural black pigments—for example, charcoal, graphite, and soot—have long been readily available for drawing, painting, and writing, a colorfast black dye proved much more elusive. Black dyes made from vegetable sources tended to fade fairly rapidly to gray. The exception was the dye made from the heartwood of logwood, a species of tree native to the Caribbean. To create a fade-resistant black fabric using dye from logwood, the cloth had to be dyed with indigo first.

PAINT
IT
BLACK

Left Alternating black treads and white risers makes a powerful statement on a staircase and adds dynamism to the views from one level to the next.

Below In the right context, black décor can be rich and dramatic, as illustrated by this study area. Many paint manufacturers now produce near-black or blue-black paints.

From painted detail to patterned fabric, there are many ways of using black within decorative schemes. The more reflective the material or finish, the greater the graphic punch.

❋
Black backgrounds
Walls tiled with black slate make dramatic backgrounds in small, enclosed areas, such as wet rooms or bathrooms. A portion of a wall painted with chalkboard paint makes a handy place to write up reminders in kitchens or utility areas, or for creative scribbling in children's rooms.

❋
Black floors
For added definition underfoot, and to serve as an anchor for decorative schemes, choose black flooring: glossy ebonized floorboards, slate tiles, or black-dyed natural-fiber matting. Like white surfaces, however, black flooring will show up every speck of dust.

❋
Black details
Black marble or granite work surfaces underscore the architectural detail of built-in kitchens and bathrooms. Black paint is also a traditional choice for hearths and iron fire surrounds. Black leather upholstery emphasizes the contours of seat furniture.

❋
Black and white
This traditional pairing crops up in a wide range of designs and patterns, both historic and contemporary, from black-and-white checkered flooring in marble and slate, to bold striped rugs and weaves.

Below Black as a dominant shade in the interior can be a little easier to handle underfoot. Black wood, stone, matting, or carpet are all options, as is the striped rug seen here.

Right This chevron-patterned black-and-white tiled floor has an almost optical effect, reminiscent of the paintings of Bridget Riley. The glossy black headboard, rippled black-and-white seat upholstery, and display of black-and-white photographs pursue the strong graphic theme.

GRAY

Left Schemes based around shades of gray don't have to be dreary or banal. A great deal depends on texture. Here the smooth polished-concrete floor contrasts with the softer gray upholstery weaves. What really brings it all to life is the shiny copper tray table.

Below Midblue cups and tableware sing out against the tones of gray that have been used to decorate this plain and unassuming dining area.

The color of shadows, fog, and overcast days, gray has its fair share of negative associations, from boredom and conformity to uncertainty and drabness. Lacking the airy freshness of white and the graphic punch of black, at first glance gray seems neither one thing nor the other. In nature, it is prevalent as camouflage—gray fur, gray feathers, and gray skin allow creatures to blend with their backgrounds. Its widespread modern use in soulless corporate environments and dreary concrete cityscapes hasn't helped its image, either.

Yet gray is actually a very versatile family of shades and, according to a recent newspaper article, a newly fashionable one, both in clothing and interiors—an increase in sales of gray paint reported by leading manufacturers would seem to bear this out. Gray may well be reticent and unassuming, but it invites us to look beneath the surface and explore material quality. Textural grays, expressed in natural weaves, limed wood, and stone, have both stability and an understated luxury.

The obvious way to make gray is to mix white and black together in different proportions. This gives a gradation of tonalities, from the palest whisper of velvety dove-gray to the deep shades of anthracite and battleship-gray. More complex and interesting grays, however, come from the blend of two complementary colors, such as red and green.

Below Hans Wegner's PP19 design, or Teddy Bear Chair (1951), is an icon of modern Danish design. Gray upholstery is particularly effective in natural or tweedy weaves.

Right The mottled gray wall finish, woodwork, and bed linen create an atmosphere of rest and repose.

SHADES OF GRAY

Left This elegant contemporary scheme in white, gray, and black relies on the integrity and texture of natural materials for its impact. The chairs are Arne Jacobsen's Ant 3010 design, dating from 1952.

Below Gray flooring in stone, tile or painted wood has infinitely more character than featureless swathes of gray fitted carpet. The spindle-backed chair is Mademoiselle (1956), a classic Finnish design by Ilmari Tapiovaara.

Depending on the precise mix, a particular shade of gray will tend to either the cool or warm end of the spectrum. Whichever is the case, gray's natural tendency to be recessive means that it combines well with almost any other color. Blue-grays, gray-greens, gray-browns, and grays with a hint of purple or yellow are all intriguing, refined shades that shift in tone with changing light levels. I'm glad to say that we've included many of these subtle colors in our new paint range.

BACKGROUNDS

Almost all shades of gray make very elegant backgrounds that are less stark than white and less dominant than the more attention-seeking colors in the spectrum. There are no overt historical overtones, which means they suit all styles of decoration, from country to contemporary. Gray also has the ability to enhance other colors; set stronger shades against gray walls and the effect is supremely sophisticated.

✻ Because gray doesn't draw the eye, it can be a useful remedial tool in decoration. A low ceiling that is painted gray, for example, will be less obvious than one that is painted white.

✻ Gray flooring may call to mind featureless expanses of gray carpeting in office interiors, but it doesn't have to be that way. Natural materials, such as certain kinds of limestone, slate, and limed-wood finishes, have such textural depth that the result is never bland. Alternatively, look out for flecked or mottled grays—pepper-and-salt Berber carpeting, for example, has inherent liveliness.

DETAILS

Gray's role as a mediator and enhancer of other colors is evident when it is used for details. Dark grays work like black to give color combinations definition and outline. Light grays work like white to introduce a feeling of spaciousness.

Gray is a shadowy color that appears only partly lit. This makes it useful for concealment or the type of three-dimensional modeling that is sometimes required in built-in spaces. A gray plinth or baseboard underneath white kitchen cabinets, for example, will not only show less superficial wear and tear, but will also recede into the background, making a more visually comfortable junction with the floor. Similarly pale-gray woodwork makes an elegant foil for more brightly colored or patterned walls.

Gray upholstery and soft furnishings help to prevent large-scale seat furniture from appearing overly dominating. Textured weaves, from undyed wool to herringbone and tweed, have depth of character.

This page In the study at my apartment in London, a collection of monochromatic ceramics are displayed on cantilevered shelves in shades that deepen from white at the top, through pale to dark gray, to black at the bottom.

METALLICS

Left Liveliest of all grays are metallic finishes, with their reflective sheen. This brushed-steel island unit has a soft, tactile quality.

Below left Stripping the original finishes off vintage or reclaimed office furniture transforms it into sleek contemporary pieces, such as this storage locker.

Below right Stainless steel takes a bit of care and effort to keep its handsome looks.

Gray is notionally the color of a range of metallic finishes seen on details around the home, from chrome- or nickel-plated faucets, door handles, window fittings or catches to more expansive brushed-stainless-steel surfaces. Unlike brass and bronze, which have traditional or period overtones, gray or silvery details are instantly contemporary. Not long ago we changed all the porcelain doorknobs at our house in the country to nickel-plated ones and the effect was to inject a fresh new sense of modernity.

Professional-style kitchens, with their stainless-steel worktops and appliances, have an appealing no-nonsense quality. While there's a certain degree of upkeep required to keep such finishes looking their best, the lively reflective quality means there is no hint of dullness.

CLASSIC
CONRAN
COLOR
PURE WHITE

Pure white is something of an absolute—theoretically, it is the color of light, which contains all colors. Over the centuries the search for a pure-white pigment saw the use of many different ingredients, some of them highly toxic, such as lead. The arrival of titanium white in the early part of the 20th century brought a bright opaque white into general use for the first time.

The domestic epitome of pure white is bone china, until recently almost exclusively an English product, first developed in the 18th century by potters such as Spode and Wedgwood. Bone china is a kind of porcelain made of bone ash, kaolin, and materials derived from feldspar. What enhances its high level of whiteness is its translucency. Because light is able to penetrate the body of a piece of bone china—plate, bowl, or cup—the whiteness has an added delicacy. In addition, the high strength of bone china means such pieces can be very thin, which contributes further to the sense of refinement. Drinking tea from a bone china cup is a very different experience to drinking from an earthenware mug.

I much prefer pure white tableware to any other kind. For me, the focus of any mealtime should be the food on the plate, not the plate itself. How food looks is as appetizing as how it smells and how it tastes—we eat first with our eyes, as the saying goes. The bone china pictured here was designed by my son Jasper for Wedgwood.

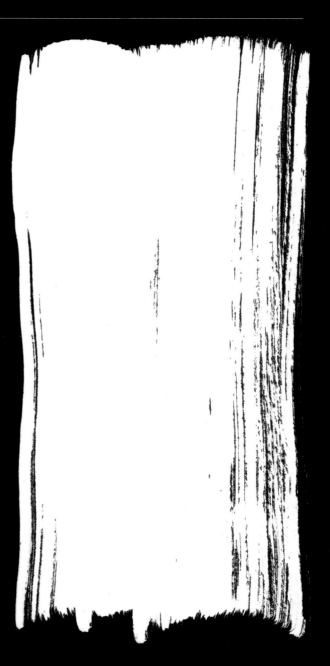

RESOURCES

See websites for store locations and outlets

DECORATIVE ELEMENTS

Cool Tiles
Floor and wall tiles
www.cooltiles.com

Farrow and Ball
Paint and wallpaper
www.farrow-ball.com

Gracious Home
www.gracioushome.com

Hunter Douglas Shades
www.hunterdouglas.com

Janovic Paint & Decorating Center
Paint, wallpaper, and shades
janovic.com

Lucy Rose Design
Fabric, wallpaper, furniture, and rugs
www.lucyrosedesign.com

Paint by Conran
Our new paint range
www.paintbyconran.com

The Tile Shop
Floor and wall tiles
www.tileshop.com

Zoffany
Fabric, wallpaper, and paint
www.zoffany.com

FURNITURE & FURNISHINGS

Artek
Classic Finnish designs by
Aalto and Tapiovaara
artekstore.com

B&B Italia
www.bebitalia.it

The Conran Shop
www.conran.com

Crate & Barrel
www.crateandbarrel.com

Design Within Reach
www.dwr.com

Fritz Hansen
Designs by Jacobsen, Wegner, and Mathsson
www.fritzhansen.com

Home Depot
www.homedepot.com

Ikea
www.ikea.com

Knoll International
Classic designs by Eames, Saarinen, and Noguchi
www.knoll.com

Muji
www.muji.com

Pottery Barn
www.potterybarn.com

Restoration Hardware
www.restorationhardware.com

West Elm
www.westelm.com

Williams-Sonoma Home
www.williams-sonoma.com

LIGHTING

Artemide
www.artemide.com

Flos
Contemporary designs by
Castiglioni and Starck
www.flos.com

Louis Poulsen
Classic designs by Jacobsen,
Henningsen, and Panton
www.louispoulsen.com

Tom Dixon
Contemporary lights
www.tomdixon.net

VINTAGE & MID-CENTURY MODERN

Ercol
Manufacturer of 'Originals'—
designs from the 1950s and 1960s
www.ercol.com

Orla Kiely
Homewares range inspired by
mid-century modern design
www.orlakiely.com

KITCHENS & BATHROOMS

Agape
www.agapedesign.it

Bed Bath and Beyond
www.bedbathandbeyond.com

Boffi
www.boffi.com

Bulthaup
www.bulthaup.com

Dornbracht
www.dornbracht.com

Siematic
www.siematic.com

Villeroy & Boch
www.villeroy-boch.com

Waterworks
www.waterworks.com

INDEX

Italic pagination indicates captions or pictures

INDEX

CREDITS

The following photographs were specially taken for Conran Octopus by Nick Pope: 1; 82; 102; 126; 148; 166; 188 & 216

The publisher would like to thank the following photographers, agencies and architects for their kind permission to reproduce the following photographs in this book:

2 Julian Cornish –Trestrail/Media 10 Images (Andy Martin Architects); 4 Time Inc UK Content; 8 Bernard Touillon/Cote Sud (Architect: Giuliano dell'Uva); 10 Mikkel Vang/Taverne Agency; 12 Ngoc Minh Ngo/Taverne Agency; 14 Hotze Eisma/production: Linda Loenen/Taverne Agency; 15 Richard Powers (Maryam Montague www.peacockpavilions.com); 16 Jake Curtis courtesy of Conran and Partners; 17 Courtesy of Conran and Partners; 18 Magnus Anesund/Soderbergagentur; 20 - 22 Time Inc UK Content; 24 Gaelle le Boulicaut (Interior Designers: Antoine Pratels and Manish Arora); 25 Time Inc UK Content; 26 Jake Fitzjones/GAP Interiors (Designer: Oliver Peake www.oliverpeake.co.uk/Stylist: Shani Zion); 27 Bertrand Limbour/House of Pictures (Owners/Design: Natasha and Henri Charles Hermans, Polyedre); 28 Mel Yates/Media 10 Images (Ashworth Parkes Architects); 29 Fernando Guerra/View Pictures (Architect: Pedro Gadanho); 30 Gaelle le Boulicaut (Designer: Muriel Verbist); 31 Ngoc Minh Ngo/Taverne Agency; 32 Time Inc UK Content; 33 left Fran Parente (Architects: Arquitetura Paralela); 33 right Time Inc UK Content; 34 Ragnar Omarsson; 35 Pascal Francois (www.studiopomka.com); 36 left Ben Anders (Owner: Bianca Hall of Kiss Her), Artwork: Valium, 2000 by Damien Hirst © Damien Hirst and Science Ltd. All rights reserved, DACS 2014; 36 right Dana van Leeuwen/Production: Jessica Bouvy/Taverne Agency; 37 Christian Schaulin / Kerstin Rose medienservice; 38 Drew Kelly; 39 left Loga Macdougall Pope/View Pictures (Giles Pike Architects); 39 right Anouk de Kleermaeker/Taverne Agency;

40 Gaelle le Boulicaut (Deisgners: Nathalie Wolberg & Tim Stokes); 41 above Carl Dahlstedt/Living Inside; 41 below Eve Wilson (Walsh St house by Robin Boyd in Melbourne, Australia); 42 left Nathalie Krag/Production: Leonoor Ottink/Taverne Agency; 42 right Felix Odell/ Cameralink/House of Pictures (Styling: Andre Schievink/House of Pictures); 43 left Jean-Marc Palisse/Cote Paris (Designer: Caroline Clavier); 43 centre Rishi Saether/House of Pictures (Styling: Ranvita La Cour/House of Pictures); 43 right Karina Tengberg/House of Pictures (Styling by Tami Christiansen/House of Pictures Design: David Alhadeff); 44 Time Inc UK Content; 45 left Richard Powers (Architects: Kerry Hill Architects www.kerryhillarchitects.com); 45 right Anna de Leeuw/Production: Sjoukje de Vries/Taverne Agency; 46 Ditte Isager, Couresty of Made A Mano; 47 Michael Franke/Media 10 Images (Sanei Hopkins Architects); 48 Jean-Marc Palisse/Cote Paris (Designer: Elke Danet), abstract painting by Hervé Half © ADAGP, Paris and DACS, London 2014; 49 Ngoc Minh Ngo/Taverne Agency; 50 Sally Chance-H&L/House of Pictures /Styling: Anne Schauffer-H&L/House of Pictures; 52 Time Inc UK Content; 54 Gaelle le Boulicaut (Designers: www.burattibattiston.it); 56 Shirley Kilpatrick/Alamy; 58 Jonas Ingerstedt/House of Pictures (Styling and design: SAŠA ANTID); 60 Richard Powers (Florence Lopez www.florence lopez.com); 62 Alessandra Ianniello/HomeStories; 63 Edmund Sumner/View Pictures; 64 above Gaelle le Boulicaut (Designer: Francois Smillenko); 64 below Paula Red/Mainstreamimages; 65 Anouk de Kleermaeker/Production: Leonie Mooren/Taverne Agency; 66 John Dummer/Production: Kerstin Jonkers/Taverne Agency; 67 Julie Ansiau; 68 Nik Epifanidis/Taverne Agency; 69 Prue Ruscoe/

Taverne Agency; 70 Hotze Eisma/Production: Linda loenen/Taverne Agency; 71 left Time Inc UK Content; 71 right Hans Zeegers/Production: Marita Jansen/Taverne Agency; 72 Graham Atkins-Hughes; 73 above Patric Johansson/House of Pictures (Styling: Pamela Pomplitz/House of Pictures); 73 below Dan Duchars/GAP Interiors; 74 Jean-Marc Palisse/Cote Paris (Designer: Florence Lopez); 76 Courtesy of California Shutters; 77 Michael Paul/Living Inside; 78 Carl Dalsthed/Living Inside + styling; 79 left Courtesy of Pearson Lyle Management Ltd/Fired Earth © Emma Lee; 79 right Greg Cox/H&L/GAP Interiors (Stylist: Jeanne Botes); 80 Birgitta W. Drejer/Sisters Agency (Stylist: Pernille Vest, Homeowner: Marie Worsaae); 81 Alain Potignon/Maison Magazine (Architect: Emmanuelle Paris); 84 Plainview/Getty Images; 86 Ben Anders (Architects: Studiomama); 88 Jacques Dirand/The Interior Archive (Architect: Philippe Harden); 89 Dana van Leeuwen/Production: Jessica Bouvy/Taverne Agency; 90 Gaelle le Boulicaut (Designers: Nathalie Wolberg & Tim Stokes); 91 Greg Cox/H&L/GAP Interiors (Stylist: Jeanne Botes); 92 left Alessandra Ianniello/HomeStories; 92 right Mark Luscombe-Whyte/The Interior Archive, (Designer: Jason Maclean); 93 Henri Del Olmo/Côté Sud / Basset Images/House of Pictures (Styling : Caroline Guiol Decorator : Karine Striga); 94 Chris Tubbs (Interior design: Orla Kiely); 95 Courtesy of Vanessa Arbuthnott (www.vanessaarbuthnott.co.uk); 96 Darren Chung/Mainstream images; 97 Photo & Styling: Jeltje Janmaat/House of Pictures; 98 Patric Johansson/House of Pictures (Styling: Pamela Pomplitz/House of Pictures); 99 Dustin Aksland (Architect: Jeff Sherman); 100 Photo: Lisbett Wedendahl, Courtesy of Louis Poulsen; 101 Jake Fitzjones/GAP

Interiors (Designer: Jose Soto, Builder: Marco Oddi, Stylist: Shani Zion); 104 Lubos Paukeje/Alamy; 106 Christian Schaulin / Kerstin Rose medienservice; 108 Alessandra Ianniello/HomeStories; 109 Courtesy of Bruce Bolander Architect; 110-111 Gaelle le Boulicaut (Designers: Nathalie Wolberg & Tim Stokes); 112 above Time Inc UK Content; 112 below Gaelle le Boulicaut (Designers: Nathalie Wolberg & Tim Stokes); 113 Time Inc UK Content; 114 Chris Tubbs; 116 Anouk de Kleermaeker/Production: Leonie Mooren/Taverne Agency; 117 Drew Kelly; 118 Time Inc UK Content; 119 left Aleph/Eric Flogny/Marie Claire Maison/Camera Press (Owner and artist: Jean François Fourtou); 119 right Birgitta W. Drejer/Sisters Agency (Stylist Pernille Vest); 120 David Cleveland/GAP Interiors; 121 Photo & Styling: Jeltje Janmaat/House of Pictures; 122 Gaelle le Boulicaut (Archiects & Designers: Stamberg Aferiat & Ass.); 123 Time Inc UK Content; 124 Peter Margonelli/Red Cover/Photoshot; 125 Serge Anton/Living Inside; 128 Stephen Mulcahey/Alamy; 130 David Garcia; 132 Jochen Arndt/Taverne Agency; 133 Aubrey Jonsson–H&L/House of Pictures (Styling Leana Schoeman–H&L/House of Pictures); 134 Richard Powers (Design Gallery/Bulthaup, www.design-gallery.ru the apartment of Lina Perlova, head of Design Gallery/Bulthaup in Saint-Petersburg); 135 Ngoc Minh Ngo/Taverne Agency; 136 Marjon Hoogervorst/Taverne Agency; 137 Fisher Hart/View Pictures (Interior Design: Geraldine Morley); 138 Garth Oriander (Architects: Sanders & King); 139 Camera Press (Derek Swalwell/bauersyndication.com.au and DX Architects dxarchitects.com.au); 140 Jansje Klazinga/Taverne Agency; 141 Anna de Leeuw (Production: Sjoukje de Vries)/Taverne Agency; 142 Ray Main/Mainstreamimages; 143 Nathalie Krag/Production: Leonoor Ottink/Taverne Agency; 144 Elisabeth Aarhus/Mainstreamimages; 145 Fernando Guerra | FG+SG; 146 Time Inc UK Content; 147 Photo & Styling: Jeltje Janmaat/House of Pictures; 150 Javarman/Alamy; 152 & 154 Time Inc UK Content; 155 Germain Suignard/Marie Claire Maison/Camera Press (Architect: Nathalie Robin); 156 Lisa Romerein/Otto Archive; 157 Sharyn Cairns/Taverne Agency; 158 David Garcia; 159 above Time Inc UK Content; 159 below Chris Tubbs/GAP Interiors (Designer: Charles Mellersh); 160 Anna de Leeuw/Production: Sjoukje de Vries/Taverne Agency; 161 Marjon Hoogervorst/Taverne Agency; 162 Warnes and Walton/Living Inside; 163 Piotr Gesicki/GAP Interiors; 164 Simon Maxwell (Architect: Matt Architecture www.mattarchitecture.com); 165 Time Inc UK Content; 168 Gaia Moments/Alamy; 170 Time Inc UK Content; 172 Rachel Whiting/GAP Interiors; 173 & 174 Birgitta W. Drejer/Sisters Agency; 175 Birgitta W. Drejer/Sisters Agency (Stylist Pernille Vest); 176 Nicolas Mathéus / Basset Images House of Pictures (Styling : Laurence Dougier Architect : Thomas Fourtané from Achipetrus studio Interior Designer : Véronique Lecomte); 177 Anna de Leeuw/Production: Sjoukje de Vries/Taverne Agency; 178 Pascal Francois (www.studiopomka.com); 179 Prue Ruscoe/Production: Shannon Fricke/Taverne Agency; 180 Heidi Lerkenfeldt/Linnea Press; 181 Birgitta W. Drejer/Sisters Agency (www.thissionr2.com); 182 Earl Carter/Production: Annemarie Kiely/Taverne Agency; 183 Time Inc UK Content; 184 Pascal Francois (www.studio pomka.com); 185 Fabrizio Cicconi/Living Inside; 186 Martin Solyst/Erik Bjorn/Living Inside; 190 Valentyn Volkov/Alamy; 192 Richard Powers (Amansari www.aman.com, Kerry Hill Architects www.kerryhill architects.com); 194 Tommy Durath/House of Pictures (Styling: Anna Örnberg/House of Pictures); 195 left Birgitta W. Drejer/Sisters Agency; 195 right Photo & Styling: Jeltje Janmaat/House of Pictures; 196 Rachel Whiting/GAP Interiors; 197 Michael Paul/Living Inside; 198 Sameli Rantanen (Design: Ulla Koskinen), The Lato house is made by Kannustalo; 199 Photo & Styling: Jeltje Janmaat/House of Pictures; 200 Jan Baldwin/Narratives (Stylist: Margaret Caselton); 201 Per Magnus Persson/House of Pictures (Designer Jimmy Schoenning); 202 Sharyn Cairns/Taverne Agency; 203 Sally Chance-H&L/House of Pictures/Styling: Anne Schauffer-H&L/House of Pictures; 204 Courtesy of Crucial Trading; 205 Gaelle le Boulicaut (Interior Designers: Cecilia Morelli & Ashiesh Shah); 206 Jonas Bjerre-Poulsen/Norm Architects; 207 Michael Paul/Living Inside; 208 Peter Fehrentz; 209 Jean-Marc Palisse/Cote Est (Designer: Helene Roux); 210 Birgitta W. Drejer/Sisters Agency (Stylist Pernille Vest); 211 Anna de Leeuw/Production: Sjoukje de Vries/Taverne Agency; 212 Time Inc UK Content; 214 Verity Welstead/Narratives; 215 left Bjarni B. Jacobsen/Pure Public/Living Inside; 215 right A. Mezza & E. Escalante/Narratives 224 Royal Academy of Arts, London; photographer: John Hammond

Every effort has been made to trace the copyright holders. We apologise in advance for any unintentional omissions and would be pleased to insert the appropriate acknowledgement in any subsequent publication.

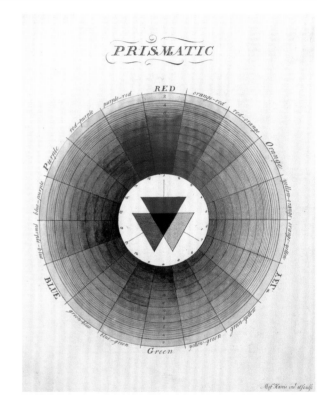

An Hachette UK Company
www.hachette.co.uk

First published in Great Britain
in 2015 by Conran Octopus Ltd,
a division of
Octopus Publishing Group Ltd
Endeavour House,
189 Shaftesbury Avenue,
London WC2H 8JY
www.octopusbooks.co.uk
www.octopusbooksusa.com

Distributed in the US by
Hachette Book Group
1290 Avenue of the Americas
4th and 5th Floors
New York, NY 10020

Distributed in Canada by
Canadian Manda Group
664 Annette St.
Toronto, Ontario, Canada M6S 2C8

ISBN 978 1 84091 685 0

Printed and bound in China

10 9 8 7 6 5 4 3 2 1

Contributing Editor:
   Elizabeth Wilhide

Publisher: Alison Starling
Design & Art Direction:
   Jonathan Christie
Senior Editor: Sybella Stephens
Editor: Zia Mattocks
Picture Researcher: Liz Boyd
Senior Production Manager:
   Katherine Hockley